World Legislatures

W0080120

World Legislatures

John Paxton

M

First published 1974 by
THE MACMILLAN PRESS LTD
London and Basingstoke
Associated companies in New York Dublin
Melbourne Johannesburg and Madras

SBN 333 14849 5

Bound by Mansell Ltd.,
Witham, Essex.

ISBN 978-1-349-27915-9   ISBN 978-1-349-27913-5 (eBook)
DOI 10.1007/978-1-349-27913-5

Contents

Contents (continued)

Contents (continued)

Contents (continued)

Page   Page

Contents (continued)

DIAGRAMS

Introduction

World Legislatures is limited in its aims. The word 'legislature' is a loose one and is very often used synonymously with 'Parliament' and 'Assembly'. In fact a considerable proportion of parliamentary time is not devoted to making laws; a far larger proportion is used to criticise the government of the day. The aim of *World Legislatures* is to concentrate, in one volume, on the processes of making laws and the process of electing the law-makers. It should be remembered, however, that the legislature may not have total power in law-making. In the USA, both at Federal and State level; the President and Governors have powers to veto Bills passed by the legislators. A study of the entries show the number of countries where the Presidents are governing without an elected Parliament and ruling by decree.

Perhaps the most interesting entry in this first edition of *World Legislatures* is the last one. This is a 'rogue' entry because the Parliament of the European Economic Community in Strasbourg has, at the time of writing, no legislative authority. In the near future it may herald a new pattern of parliamentary power. Henri Fayat, President of the Council of Ministers, has described the aim of this Parliament as 'A supranational political body endowed with executive, legislative and judicial powers'. It may be remembered that in 1965 the EEC Commission advised that the European Parliament should have wider powers and authority, but this was rejected by President de Gaulle. A decade has gone by and in the next few years Europe will witness the evolution of one of the most interesting legislative assemblies that the twentieth century has seen.

The history of parliaments is long. Government by the people, or democracy, has been practised in many ways in many places. Indeed, the use of the word 'democracy' would appear to have considerable variants of meaning. Direct democracy, as practised in some of the city-states of Greece, was uncomplicated. Indirect democracy, developed in Britain in the seventeenth century, was better suited to areas of large population. By the mid-nineteenth century a large proportion of independent nations had adopted democratic institutions. Democracy as accepted in western Europe and the USA is based on the theory of 'separation of powers'. The powers of government consist of the legislative, the executive and the judicial. Separation of power implies that none of these is able to control or interfere with the others. It also implies that individuals cannot hold posts in more than one of the three branches. It has been stated that the stability of British governments has been the separation of powers. In the USA executive power is vested in the President, and the departmental heads are responsible to him and not to Congress. In Britain changes have taken place and the executive is responsible to the legislature. The judiciary remains independent of the executive and must carry out the laws passed by the legislature.

All this implies that elections should be held at regular intervals and that the electorate should make a choice between two or more political parties. Therefore where the elections are held with only a single list of candidates for the electorate to choose or reject they cannot be considered democratic in this sense of the word.

Government by the people is used in another context in many countries of eastern Europe. The principle of the separation of powers is not generally accepted, but alternatively, in these countries, the private ownership of the means of production is regarded as undemocratic.

Legislatures differ considerably in the procedures adopted to enact laws. In democracies the starting point is the bill and, generally after a formal first reading, the bill goes to some form of committee. The committee stage of a bill receives little publicity but probably, it is at this stage that the most constructive speaking takes place. On the floor of the House speeches have a wider audience and so greater shades of party political reasoning are displayed. Bills then follow a pattern of several readings in the House in a unicameral legislature and through the lower and upper Houses in those that are bicameral. Then follows promulgation which is the act of turning the bill into law and in a monarchy is achieved by obtaining the royal assent. In some countries the right of veto exists even at this late stage. The President of the United States, for instance, is independent of Congress and retains the right of veto. Publication in the official gazette generally completes the law-making process.

The size of the legislature varies considerably but seems to, generally, range from one hundred to four hundred. This is not really the place to discuss the seating arrangements of legislatures but the largest number of legislatures seem to have been built on the basis of a semi-circle. From this, of course, has come the phraseology of describing a Member as just 'left of centre' because the spectrum of political leaning is aligned to the seating arrangements in the semi-circle.

If the British parliamentary system, which is based on two main parties, should change dramatically in the future, it is interesting to conjecture whether the seating arrangements of the British House of Commons is suitable.

Acknowledgements

My thanks are due to correspondents throughout the world, without whose help, in clarification of detail, this work would not have been possible. Gratitude goes to Evelyn Beadle, Swan Lennard Payne, Virginia Walker and Penny White for their usual superb typing and to Sheila Bryant for careful reading of the manuscript and for much constructive criticism.

It will be necessary to revise and expand *World Legislatures* from time to time and the editor will be pleased to receive constructive and informed criticism for the next edition. Accuracy has been the main aim in this compilation but if error has crept in the editor will be pleased, although sad at the time, to be informed.

Shepton Mallet
October, 1974   J.P.

World
Legislatures

Britain must be unique in that it decided, after debate, that an insufficient number of seats should be provided for the total membership of the House of Commons. When planning the rebuilding of the House of Commons following the bombing in the Second World War, Mr (later Sir) Winston Churchill said in a debate in Parliament in 1943:

'The characteristic of a Chamber formed on the lines of the House of Commons is that it should not be big enough to contain all its Members at once without overcrowding, and that there should be no question of every Member having a separate seat reserved for him. The reason for this has long been a puzzle to uninstructed outsiders, and has frequently excited the curiosity and even the criticism of new Members.

If the House is big enough to contain all its Members nine-tenths of its debates will be conducted in the depressing atmosphere of an almost empty or half-empty chamber.'

AFGHANISTAN

Under a constitution, ratified by the Grand National Assembly (*Loe Jirga*) in Sept. 1964, which took effect in Oct. 1965, Afghanistan became a parliamentary democracy in which legislative authority rests with a National Assembly of 2 Houses. Election to the House of the People (Lower House) was by direct secret ballot, whereas the House of the Elders (Upper House) was, in many cases, by the King and by the provincial councils' appointment. The legislative, executive and judicial branches of government were separated. Certain powers, such as the appointment of the Prime Minister and judges of the Supreme Court, rested with the King, who had become a constitutional monarch. This Constitution replaced that which had been in force since 1933.

Following a military coup in July 1973, Afghanistan became a Republic and a new constitution is being drafted.

ALBANIA

The legislative body is the People's Assembly (*Kuvënd Popullor*). It is elected for a 4-year term by all citizens of 18 or over by equal, direct and secret ballot in electoral districts in the ratio of one representative for every 8,000 inhabitants. It is usual for only one approved candidate to stand in each constituency. The People's Assembly elects a Chairman. It appoints special committees as necessary, including committees of investigation.

The People's Assembly elects a Presidium composed of a President, 2 Vice-Presidents, a Secretary and 10 Members. The Presidium convenes the People's Assembly for two short regular sessions each year. Extraordinary sessions of the People's Assembly may be convened by the Presidium or at the request of one-third of the Representatives. The Presidium decrees elections, promulgates and interprets laws, issues decrees, and ratifies and denounces international treaties. It is responsible to the People's Assembly and may be revoked by it before its term has run.

Elections for a new People's Assembly must be held not later than 3 months after the dissolution of the previous one. The Presidium convenes the newly-elected People's Assembly not later than 3 months after its elections, and remains in power until a new Presidium is elected.

In cases of emergency the People's Assembly may prolong its legislature beyond the normal term. It may likewise dissolve itself before the expiry of its normal term.

Bills may be introduced by the Government, the Presidium or by Representatives. To become law a Bill must be voted by a majority of Representatives at a People's Assembly sitting attended by a majority of its Members. Bills amending the Constitution may be introduced by the Government, the Presidium or by two-thirds of the Representatives, and must be voted by two-thirds of the Representatives.

ALGERIA

Algeria is a one-party state established under the 1963 Constitution. The National Assembly is the main legislative body and considerable executive power rests with the President of the Republic, acting through the Revolutionary Council. All citizens of both sexes over 19 years have the right to vote. Representatives in the National Assembly are nominated by the *Front de Liberation Nationale* (FLN).

The President of the Republic is nominated by the Party and is elected for a 5-year term by universal, direct and secret ballot. The President of the Republic and Members of the Assembly may introduce Bills. The President must promulgate laws within 10 days of their formal transmission by the National Assembly. During this period the President can request the Assembly to reconsider its decision and this request cannot be refused. In exceptional circumstances the period of 10 days can be reduced. A motion of censure can be tabled against the President by a minimum of one-third of the Members of the Assembly. If a majority vote goes against the President, he must resign and automatically there is a dissolution of the Assembly. In the case of emergency the President has the right to take measures to protect the national interest and institutions.

General elections were held in 1964 but the Assembly has not met since 1966.

ANDORRA

The political status of the co-principality of Andorra was regulated by the *Paréage* of 1278, which placed Andorra under the joint suzerainty of the Comte de Foix and of the Bishop of Urgel. The rights vested in the house of Foix passed by marriage to that of Bearn and, on the accession of Henri IV, to the French crown. The sovereignty is exercised jointly by the President of the French Republic and the Bishop of Urgel. The co-princes are represented in Andorra by the *Viguier de France* and the *Viguier Episcopal*. Each co-prince has set up a Permanent Delegation for Andorran affairs; the Prefect of the Eastern Pyrenees is the French Permanent Delegate.

A 'General Council of the Valleys' submits motions and proposals to the Permanent Delegations. Its 24 Members are elected for a 4-year term; half of the Council is renewed every 2 years. The Council nominates a First Syndic, *Syndic Procureur Général*, and a Second Syndic from outside its Members. All citizens over 21 years may vote and those over 30 years can be elected to public office.

ARGENTINA

The National Congress consists of a Senate and House of Deputies; the Senate, with 2 representatives from the capital and each province (with a total of 68 seats), elected by popular vote for 9 years (one-third retiring every 3 years). The House of Deputies was to have 243 seats, each Deputy being elected for a 4-year term and half the seats renewable each 2 years.

Since 1912 voting has been free, secret and obligatory. Women were enfranchised in Sept. 1947; beginning with the presidential election in Nov. 1951, all women 18 years or older must vote. Equal suffrage was confirmed by a revisionary law of Aug. 1961.

The provinces have extensive powers in internal matters. Each province has its own Chamber of Senators and House of Deputies.

The Constitution can be amended by Congress provided it has a two-thirds majority, and immediately a constitutional assembly must be convened.

Constitutional changes, announced in a Basic Statute in Aug. 1972, included the following. Deputies and Senators would have a 4-year mandate and could be re-elected indefinitely. Each province would be represented by 3 Senators, 2 for the majority and 1 for the minority. Both the President and the Vice-President would be elected by direct popular vote for a 4-year term, and are not eligible for a second term; and the Basic Statute would remain in force until May 1977 and could be extended for another 4 years, unless modified or incorporated permanently in the Constitution by a special constitutional committee.

Further constitutional changes were contained in an electoral law promulgated in Oct. 1972. Under this law the President and the Vice-President would be elected together (and no longer, as hitherto, by a college of electors making its choice a fortnight after general elections); if no party obtained 51 per cent of the votes cast, there would follow a second 'run-off' election, for which only the 2 strongest parties (or alliances) would be able to nominate candidates, and in which the President and Vice-President would be elected by a simple majority; if in the first election the 2 strongest parties together obtained less than 66 per cent of the votes cast, they would be allowed to enter into an alliance with any political group which had obtained at least 15 per cent of the total vote; alternatively, they would be able to form a coalition for which any party with 15 per cent of the votes in the first ballot would be eligible. Election by a simple majority would also apply to Deputies, Senators and Provincial Governors (who had previously been elected by proportional representation). In the Chamber of Deputies no party would be represented unless it gained 8 per cent, or 135,000 votes, of the total of votes cast.

AUSTRALIA

Legislative power in the Commonwealth of Australia is vested in a Federal Parliament, consisting of the Queen, represented by a Governor-General, a Senate and a House of Representatives. Under the terms of the Constitution there must be a session of Parliament at least once a year.

The Senate comprises 60 Senators (10 for each state voting as one electorate) chosen for 6 years. In general, the Senate is renewed to the extent of one-half every 3 years, but in case of prolonged disagreement with the

House of Representatives, it, together with the House of Representatives, may be dissolved and an entirely new Senate elected. The House of Representatives consists, as nearly as may be, of twice as many Members as there are Senators, the numbers chosen in the several states being in proportion to population as shown by the latest statistics, but not less than 5 for any original state. The numerical size of the House after the election in 1969 was 125, including the Members for Northern Territory and the Australian Capital Territory. The Northern Territory has been represented by 1 member in the House of Representatives since 1922, and the Australian Capital Territory by 1 Member since 1949. The Member for the Australian Capital Territory was given full voting rights as from the Parliament elected in Nov. 1966. The Member for the Northern Territory was given full voting rights in 1968. The House of Representatives continues for 3 years from the date of its first meeting, unless dissolved sooner. Every Senator or Member of the House of Representatives must be a British subject, be of full age, possess electoral qualifications and have resided for 3 years within Australia. The franchise for both Chambers is the same and is based on universal adult (at 18 years) suffrage. Compulsory voting was introduced in 1925. If a Member of a state Parliament wishes to be a candidate in a federal election, he must first resign his state seat.

Formally, executive power in the Commonwealth is vested in the Governor-General, who is advised by an Executive Council. This is presided over by the Governor-General, and its Members hold office at his pleasure. All Ministers of State are *ex-officio* Members of the Executive Council. Meetings are formal and official in character, and a record of proceedings is kept by the secretary or clerk. At Executive Council meetings the decisions of the Cabinet are (where necessary) given legal form, appointments made, resignations accepted, proclamations issued, and regulations and the like enacted.

The policy of a Ministry is, in practice, determined by the Ministers of State, meeting without the Governor-General, under the chairmanship of the Prime Minister. This group, known as the Cabinet, does not form part of the legal mechanism of government; its meetings are private and deliberative; the actual Ministers of the day are alone present; no records of the meetings are made public, and the decisions taken have, in themselves, no legal effect.

From Jan. 1956 the composition of the Ministry consisted of a Cabinet, including a limited number of Ministers, and a group of Ministers not in the Cabinet who could be invited to attend Cabinet meetings whenever matters affecting their departments are being considered. In Jan. 1973 all members of the Ministry became Cabinet Members.

The legislative powers of the Federal Parliament embrace commerce, shipping, etc.; finance, banking, currency, etc.; defence; external affairs; postal, telegraph and like services; census and statistics; weights and measures; copyright; railways; conciliation and arbitration in industrial disputes extending beyond the limits of any one state; social services (an amendment to the Constitution in 1946 specifying, in addition to the existing provision for invalid and old-age pensions, the provision of maternity allowances, widows' pensions, child endowment, unemployment, pharmaceutical, sickness and hospital benefits, medical and dental services, etc.). The Senate may not originate or amend money Bills; and disagreement with the House of Representatives may result in dissolution or, in the last resort, a joint sitting of the two Houses. No religion may be established by the Commonwealth. The Federal Parliament has limited and enumerated powers, the several state Parliaments retaining the residuary power of government over their respective territories. If a state law is inconsistent with a Commonwealth law, the latter prevails.

The Constitution also provides for the admission or creation of new states. Proposed laws for the alteration of the Constitution must be submitted to the electors, and they can be enacted only if approved by a majority of the states and by a majority of all the electors voting.

THE STATES AND TERRITORIES OF AUSTRALIA

The Governor of the individual states assents in the Sovereign's name to laws passed by State Parliaments. In all but 2 states the laws are enacted in the name of the Sovereign by, and with the consent of, the Legislative Council and Legislative Assembly. In South Australia and Tasmania laws are enacted in the name of the Governor with the advice and consent of the Parliament (South Australia), or the Legislative Council and House of Assembly (Tasmania). Bills go to a first reading with no debate. The second reading is for discussion, clause by clause, in principle, by committee of the whole. At the third reading, the general principles are reconsidered after committee amendments. No measure which has been passed by an outright majority in the Lower House may be rejected outright in the Upper.

New South Wales

New South Wales has had responsible government since 1856. Some important dates have been: manhood suffrage, 1858; principle of one elector, one vote established, 1894; Women's Franchise Act, 1902; compulsory enrolment, 1921; experiment in proportional representation for elections to Legislative Assembly, 1920–5, abandoned in 1925; compulsory voting, 1930; Legislative Council fully elective, 1934.

The Legislative Assembly has 96 Members. Elected for a 3-year term by universal suffrage of those over 21 years, subject to usual residence requirements. The Legislative Council has 60 Members. They are elected by the Members of the Legislative Assembly and Legislative Council in simultaneous session for a 12-year term; every 3 years 15 of them retire and are replaced. For the Legislative Assembly any person entitled to vote may be elected, and for the Legislative Council, any person entitled to vote for the Legislative Assembly Members. All need three years' residence in Australia.

Provision for resolving deadlock between the Houses exists but has never been used. In theory Upper House may delay money Bills for only 1 month, after which they become law without its assent. For other Bills a deadlock is resolved by a referendum of those qualified to vote for the Legislative Assembly. The Legislative Assembly has no standing committees on legislation. Very few Bills originate in the Legislative Council.

Northern Territory

The Legislative Council for the Northern Territory was set up by an amendment to the Northern Territory (Administration) Act in 1947. The Council was reconstituted in 1959, by a further amendment to the Act, to consist of the Administrator, 6 official Members, 3 appointed non-official Members and 8 elected Members. In 1965 an amendment provided for the withdrawal of the Administrator and the election of a Council President from among the elected Members. The Council was again reconstituted in 1968 to consist of 6 official and 11 elected Members, with effect from the elections for the Council held in Oct. 1968.

All Ordinances passed by the Council are presented to the Administrator for assent. The Administrator must reserve certain Ordinances for the Governor-General's pleasure. Others he may assent to, withhold assent, reserve for the Governor-General's pleasure or return to the Council with amendments that he recommends. The Governor-General may assent to an Ordinance, withhold assent to whole or part of an Ordinance, or return it to the Administrator with any amendments that he recommends. He may also disallow in whole or part any Ordinance the Administrator has assented to. All Ordinances must be laid before each House of Parliament.

An Administrator's Council was set up in 1959 to advise the Administrator on any matter referred to it by the Administrator, or in accordance with any Ordinance. The Council consists of the Administrator and 2 official and 3 elected Members of the Legislative Council.

The Northern Territory elects a Member to the House of Representatives who has full voting rights. Prior to 1968 the Member had been able to vote only on matters relating solely to the Northern Territory. Between 1922 and 1936 the Northern Territory Member had no vote.

Queensland

Queensland became a colony with responsible government in 1859, the Constitution providing two Houses, the Lower elected on a wider suffrage than the Upper. Some important dates have been: women were enfranchised by the Elections Amendment Acts, 1905 and 1907; compulsory voting, 1915;

preferential voting was abolished 1942–63; abolition of the Upper House, 1922.

There are 78 Members of the one remaining House, elected on universal adult suffrage for a 3-year term from 3 electoral districts. There are single-member constituencies. Any qualified voter may be elected a Member provided that he is not a minister of religion.

South Australia

South Australia has had a partially elective Legislative Council since 1851. Responsible government was achieved in 1856 with the establishment of 2 Houses. The Upper House was elected on narrower franchise than the Lower, which was elected on manhood suffrage. Two important dates are: Constitution Amendment Act gave women the vote, 1894; compulsory voting, 1944. The 20 Members of the Legislative Council are elected for a 6-year term, half retiring every 3. They are elected by all over 18 years with residence qualifications, who are also qualified by property or service. Members must be over 30 years with 3 years' residence.

The 47 Members of the Legislative Assembly are elected for 3 years, in single-member constituencies. Voters are all over 18 years with usual residence qualifications. Members must be qualified voters and not ministers of religion.

In the event of a deadlock between two Houses, the Governor may dissolve the Lower House. If the deadlock persists he may grant a double dissolution or issue writs for 10 new Members of the Legislative Council. This procedure has never been used.

Tasmania

Important dates in the development of the legislature of Tasmania are: Legislative Council established, partially elective, 1851; responsible government established with 2 Houses, both elective, 1856; Constitution Amendment Act gave women the vote, 1903, proportional representation introduced, 1907; compulsory voting, 1928.

The 35 Members of the Legislative Assembly are elected for a 5-year term, and elected by all over 21 years with usual residence qualifications. The constituencies have 7 Members. Casual vacancies in the House of Assembly are determined by a transfer of the preference of the vacating Member's ballot papers to consenting candidates who were unsuccessful at the last general election. Members must be qualified electors. The 19 Members of the Legislative Council are elected for a 6-year term, 3 retiring annually and 4 every sixth year. They must be qualified electors of at least 25 years, with residence qualifications. Tasmania has no formal machinery for resolving a deadlock in the legislature.

Victoria

Some important dates have been: Victoria became a colony with a Legislative Council partly elective on a narrow franchise, 1851; responsible government achieved, Constitution providing 2 Houses, the Legislative Assembly being wholly elective on a wide franchise, with single voting (introduced in 1899 (Legislative Assembly) and 1937 (Legislative Council)), 1856; manhood suffrage, 1857; Adult Suffrage Act gave women the vote, 1908; preferential voting introduced, 1911; compulsory voting for the Legislative Assembly, 1926; compulsory voting for Legislative Council, 1935; the Legislative Council elected on universal suffrage (prior to 1950, the Legislative Council was elected on limited suffrage but by a qualified section of the Legislative Assembly electorate), 1950.

The 73 Members of the Legislative Assembly are elected for a 3-year term on universal suffrage of all over 21 years with usual residence qualifications. Members must be qualified electors and not be clergymen or judges.

The 36 Members of the Legislative Council are elected for a 6-year term, half of them retiring every third year. The qualifications are the same as for the Legislative Assembly. Voting for both Houses is by preferential vote and is compulsory.

The Legislative Council may not initiate money Bills or amend them. It may suggest amendments which do not increase any proposed charge. Bills must pass both Houses to become law. A deadlock may be resolved by the Governor dissolving the Lower and then the Upper House and calling a joint sitting. This procedure has never been used.

Western Australia

In 1890 two Chambers were established, the Upper one being nominated by the Governor. There was provision that, should the population reach 60,000, the Upper Chamber should be elective, and this was achieved in 1893. Two important dates are: Constitution Acts' Amendment Act gave women the vote, 1899; compulsory voting for Legislative Assembly was established, 1936. The 30 Members of the Legislative Council are elected for a 6-year term, one-half retiring every 3 years. Two Members are returned for every electoral province. Members must be at least 18 years and be qualified electors. They must not be ministers of religion or certain officials. Electors must be over 18 years with usual residence qualifications. Enrolment is compulsory for all sectors except aborigines, but they may enrol if they wish.

The 51 Members of the Legislative Assembly are elected for a 3-year term. There is 1 Member for each electoral district. Qualifications for Members and for electors are as for the Legislative Council. Western Australia has no formal machinery for resolving a deadlock between Houses.

AUSTRIA

The legislative bodies are the *Nationalrat* (National Council) and the *Bundesrat* (Federal Council). The *Nationalrat* consists of 165 Delegates who are elected for 25 constituencies by equal, direct and secret ballot on the proportional representation system. All Austrian citizens, male and female, who are over 19 years, have the vote. Candidates for election must be over 25 years. The provinces are represented in the *Bundesrat* by 54 Delegates elected by the provincial diets in proportion to the size of the population of the various provinces. Every statute passed by the *Nationalrat* must obtain the approval of the *Bundesrat*. *Nationalrat* and *Bundesrat* together form the National Assembly, whose final approval is required in certain contingencies. A declaration of war, for instance, could only be voted by the National Assembly and could not be made effective without the approval of both Houses of Parliament. A Parliamentary term is 4 years.

The Federal President and the Federal Government are the executive authority. The President is elected by the people, by general, equal and secret ballot, for a 6-year term. He represents the Republic, convokes and prorogues Parliament, and appoints the Chancellor and his Ministers. He also signs treaties and receives an oath of allegiance from the provincial governors. He can dissolve the *Nationalrat,* but not more than once for the same reason; and federal laws become valid as soon as they receive his signature. The President also exercises supreme authority over the Austrian armed forces. If the President is for any reason temporarily unable to discharge his duties, or in the event of his death, his functions are taken over by the Chancellor If the President's incapacity seems likely to exceed a period of 20 days, the main committee of the *Nationalrat* nominates one or more persons to deputise for him.

The President appoints the Chancellor and, at the latter's suggestion, the Ministers. Any citizen over 29 years and legally eligible for membership of the *Nationalrat* can be appointed a Minister, but the Federal Ministers need not be Deputies of the *Nationalrat.* According to the Constitution, the Federal President is completely free in his choice of Cabinet Members. Since, however, the Federal Chancellor and the individual Federal Ministers cannot exercise their functions if they do not enjoy the confidence of the majority of Deputies in the *Nationalrat,* only such persons can be nominated as Ministers who enjoy the confidence of the majority in Parliament. The Members of the Cabinet are responsible to the *Nationalrat* for the performance of their functions and for the activities of their subordinate officials. According to the Constitution, a Minister who receives a vote of no confidence must be relieved of his office.

Each of the 9 federal provinces is administered by a provincial government headed by a provincial governor elected by the Diet. Members of the Diets are elected according to the same principles as Members of *Nationalrat*. The number of Deputies in the Diets varies with the number of inhabitants of the province concerned. Subordinate to the provincial governments are, as administrative bodies, the prefectures (*Bezirkshauptmaṇnschaften*) composed of civil servants, and also the municipal authorities, responsible to elected municipal councillors. The municipal councillors elect the mayors of towns, parishes, and villages.

Bills may be initiated by either House or by the government but must be presented in the National Council. There is provision also for the popular initiative; every proposal signed by 200,000 *Länder* voters or half the voters in each of the three *Länder* must be submitted to the National Council. The National Council may also request a referendum on a Bill which it has assented to. All Bills go secondly to the Federal Council which may object to them within 8 weeks; the Bill becomes law if the National Council reaffirms it with half its members present.

THE COMMONWEALTH OF THE BAHAMAS

Internal self-government with Cabinet responsibility was introduced on 7 Jan. 1964 and the Bahamas became independent in 1973. There is a Senate of 16 Members and a House of Assembly of 38 elected Members. Nine Senators are appointed by the Governor on the advice of the Premier, 4 on the advice of the Leader of the Opposition and 3 at the Governor's discretion. The General Assembly Elections Act, 1959, as amended, provides for universal adult suffrage. Persons of 18 years and over who hold Bahamian citizenship are eligible to vote. The House normally has a 5-year term, but it may be dissolved at any time by the Governor on the advice of the Prime Minister.

BAHRAIN

The ruling family, the Al Khalifah, an Arab dynasty, has been in power since 1782. The present ruler is also Prime Minister. The Council of State was abolished in 1971. In Dec. 1972 the first Constituent Assembly was elected and a new Constitution was published in 1973 and the first elections to the National Assembly were held in Dec. 1973. The 30 Members are elected for a 4-year term by male adult (20 years) suffrage. Members must be 30 years and have been Bahraini citizens for 15 years. In addition 12 Cabinet Ministers are members of the National Assembly. There are no political parties and candidates stand in their individual capacity.

BANGLADESH

The President of Bangladesh, who is elected by Members of Parliament in accordance with the provisions of the Constitution, is the Head of State and in exercise of all his functions he acts in accordance with the advice of the Prime Minister.

Under the Constitution executive authority of the Republic is exercised by or on the authority of the Prime Minister. Parliament (*Jatiya Sangsad*) consists of a unicameral legislature with 315 seats. Fifteen seats are reserved for women. Voting for Members of Parliament is by universal adult (18 years or over) suffrage and Members are elected for a 5-year term, unless the Government resigns or a vote of no confidence is passed.

Any clause of the Constitution can be amended or repealed by Act of Parliament, but this needs a two-thirds majority of the total number of the Members.

BARBADOS

Full internal self-government was attained in 1961 and Barbados became independent in Nov. 1966. The legislature consists of the Governor-General, a Senate and a House of Assembly. The Senate comprises 21 Members appointed by the Governor-General, 12 are appointed on the advice of the Prime Minister, 2 on the advice of the Leader of the Opposition and 7 in the Governor-General's discretion. The House of Assembly comprises 24 Members elected for a 5-year term by adult (18 years or over) suffrage.

BELGIUM

The Constitution of 1831 established Belgium as a constitutional, representative and hereditary monarchy. The legislative power is vested in the King, the Senate and the Chamber of Representatives. The royal succession is in direct male line in the order of primogeniture. By marriage without the King's consent, however, the right of succession is forfeited, but may be restored by the King with the consent of the two Chambers. No act of the King can have effect unless countersigned by one of his Ministers, who thus becomes responsible for it. The King convokes, prorogues and dissolves the Chambers. In default of male heirs, the King may nominate his successor with the consent of the Chambers. If the successor be under 18 years, the two Chambers meet together for the purpose of nominating a regent during the minority.

Those sections of the Belgian Constitution which regulate the organisation of the legislative power were revised in Oct. 1921. For both Senate and Chamber all elections are held on the principle of universal suffrage.

The Senate consists of Members elected for 4 years, partly directly and partly indirectly. The number elected directly is equal to half the number of Members of the Chamber of Representatives. The constituent body is similar to that which elects Deputies to the Chamber; the minimum age of electors is 21 years and the minimum length of residence required is 6 months. Women were given the suffrage at parliamentary elections in 1948. In the direct elections of Members, both of the Senate and Chamber of Representatives, the principle of proportional representation was introduced by a law of 1899.

Senators are elected indirectly by the provincial councils, on the basis of 1 for 200,000 inhabitants. Every addition of 125,000 inhabitants gives the right to 1 extra Senator. Each provincial council elects at least 3 Senators. There are at present 48 provincial Senators. No one, during 2 years preceding the election, must have been a member of the council appointing him. Senators are elected by the Senate itself in the proportion of half the preceding category. The Senators belonging to these two latter categories are also elected by the method of proportional representation. All Senators must be at least 40 years of age. Sons of the King, or failing these, Belgian princes of the reigning branch of the royal family, are by right Senators at the age of 18 years, but have no voice in the deliberations till the age of 25 years; this prerogative is hardly ever used.

The Members of the Chamber of Representatives are elected directly by the electoral body. Their number, at present 212 (law of 3 Apr. 1965), is proportional to the population and cannot exceed 1 for every 40,000 inhabitants. They sit for 4 years. Deputies must be not less than 25 years and resident in Belgium.

With a few minor exceptions, the House of Representatives and Senate are equally competent. The three bodies forming the legislative power have an equal right of initiative, meaning that they are empowered to table draft legislation and bills; they are competent to exercise control over public finances and to exercise control over the formation, the policy and the resignation of the Government. They are also competent in a whole range of special matters which are generally considered as the acts of the supreme authority. These include the designation of a Regent of the Realm in case of necessity; the granting of Belgian naturalisation; the determination of the strength of the armed forces, etc. To enable Members of Parliament to accomplish the tasks entrusted to them in the proper manner, a certain number of privileges have been granted them: the right to question Ministers; the right to ask questions in Parliament; the right to demand enquiries; and the right to Parliamentary immunity.

The Senate and Chamber meet annually in October and must sit for at least 40 days. The King has the power of convoking extraordinary sessions and of dissolving them either simultaneously or separately. In the latter case a new election must take place within 40 days, and a meeting of the Chambers within 2 months. An adjournment cannot be made for a period exceeding 1 month without the consent of the Chambers.

BELIZE

Under the 1964 Constitution, Belize, formerly British Honduras, has a 2-chamber legislature, with a ministerial system and cabinet responsibility. The House of Representatives consists of 18 Members elected by universal suffrage. The Senate consists of 8 Members, 5 of whom are appointed on the advice of the Premier, 2 on the advice of the Leader of the Opposition and 1 by the Governor.

The Governor retains responsibility for defence, external affairs, internal security, the safeguarding of conditions of service of public officers, and also over finance 'so long as the Government of Belize is in receipt of budgetary aid from the British Government'.

BERMUDA

Bermuda is a colony with representative government. Under the Constitution of 1968 the Governor, appointed by the Crown, is normally bound to accept the advice of the Executive Council in matters other than external affairs, defence, internal security and the police, for which he retains special responsibility. The Executive Council is appointed from among Members of the bicameral legislature, on the recommendation of the Government Leader. The Legislative Council, of whom 1 or 2 Members may serve on Executive Council, consists of 11 Members; 5 are appointed in the discretion of the Governor, 4 on the recommendation of the Government Leader and 2 on the recommendation of the Opposition Leader. The 40 Members of the House of Assembly are elected 2 from each of 20 constituencies by universal suffrage at 21 years. Candidates for election must qualify as electors and in addition must possess Bermudan status.

BHUTAN

In 1907 the Tongsa Penlop (the Governor of the province of Tongsa in eastern Bhután), Sir Ugyen Wangchuk, GCIE, KCSI, was elected as the first hereditary Maharaja of Bhután.

From 1969 the absolute monarchy was changed to a form of 'democratic monarchy', the powers of removal and selection of the King having been given to the National Assembly (*Tsogdu*). The monarch can be removed by a two-thirds vote of the Assembly Members at any time. A vote of confidence in the King, by a two-thirds majority, is required every 3 years. New monarchs would be appointed by the Assembly from the line of succession of members of the royal family. The National Assembly was made sovereign with the right to outvote any government Bills or proposals of the King. All adults over 17 years have the right to vote.

BOLIVIA

Congress consists of 2 Chambers, a Senate and a Chamber of Deputies, and meets for 90 days a year, which can be extended to 120 days. Each of the 9 departments elects 3 Senators to serve for a 4-year term. One-third of the Senate retires every 2 years. The 102 Deputies are elected for a 4-year term. 61 Deputies retire every 2 years.

All citizens over 21 years, whether literate or not, may vote.

BOTSWANA

The executive rests with the President of the Republic, who is responsible to the National Assembly. The National Assembly consists of 36 Members, 32 elected by universal suffrage at 21 years, 4 specially elected, and the Attorney-General *ex-officio*.

The President is an *ex-officio* Member of the Assembly. If the President is already a Member of the National Assembly, a by-election is held in the constituency of that Member. There is also a House of Chiefs to advise the Government. It consists of the Chiefs of the 8 principal tribes as *ex-officio* Members and 4 Members elected by and from among the sub-Chiefs in 4 districts.

The President has powers to delay implementation of legislature for 6 months and certain matters have to be referred to the House of Chiefs for approval. The House of Chiefs has no power of veto.

BRAZIL

The 1967 Constitution (amended 1969) stated that Brazil was a Federative Republic, consisting of 22 states, one federal district and territories, indissolubly united under a representative form of government to constitute the Union. The authority of the Union derives from the people and is exercised in their name and on their behalf by the legislative branches acting in co-operation, but working as autonomous bodies. The Constitution provides that the legislative power is exercised by the National Congress, which is composed of the Chamber of Deputies and the Federal Senate.

The Chamber of Deputies is elected in proportion to population in the states, the federal district and the territories. The number of Deputies is fixed in the following proportion: 1 for each 300,000 inhabitants, and beyond this limit, 1 for every million inhabitants. Each territory has 1 Deputy, and the minimum number for each state is 7.

The Federal Senate is elected by the majority principle on the basis of 3 Senators for each State. The senatorial mandate lasts 8 years. The representation of each State is renewed every 4 years, alternately, by one third and two thirds.

Voting is compulsory for all citizens between 18 and 65 years, and optional for those over 65 years. Enlisted men and illiterates (who comprise 40 per cent of the population) may not vote.

The Congress meets in the capital of the Republic from 1 Mar. to 30 June, and from 1 Aug. to 30 Nov.

Executive power is exercised by the President of the Republic, who is elected for a 4-year term. The Vice-President is elected at the same time, and he succeeds the President if the post becomes vacant. The President is assisted by a Cabinet composed of Ministers of State.

Candidates for the Presidency must be Brazilian-born citizens in full enjoyment of all their civil rights, and over 35 years. The President is elected by simple majority in open session, by an electoral college composed of all Members of the Federal Congress and of Delegates appointed by the State Legislatures, on the basis of 3 for each state and 1 more for each 500,000 voters registered in the state. The President is not eligible for re-election.

The states of the Federation have their own government with powers in all matters not specifically reserved for the Union or assigned to the Municipal Councils under the Federal Constitution. Each state has its own legislature (State Assembly), the Members of which are elected by popular vote.

BRITISH VIRGIN ISLANDS

The Governor is responsible for defence and internal security, external affairs, the public service, the courts and finance. The Executive Council consists of the Governor, 2 *ex-officio* Members and 3 Ministers from the legislature. The Legislative Council consists of 2 official Members, 1 nominated Member and 7 elected Members, from 7 one-member electoral districts; the Speaker is elected from outside the Council.

BRUNEI

The 1965 Constitution provided a Privy Council, a Council of Ministers and a Legislative Council. The Legislative Council is presided by a Speaker and consists of 6 *ex-officio* Members, 5 nominated Members and 10 elected Members. The Council of Ministers is presided by the Sultan and consists of 6 *ex-officio* Members, the High Commissioner and 4 other Members, all of whom are Members of the Legislative Council. The Mentri Besar, who is one of the *ex-officio* Members of the Legislative Council and the Council of Ministers, is responsible to the Sultan for the exercise of executive authority in the State.

BULGARIA

The legislature is the National Assembly (*Narodno Sŭbranie*). The Constitution states that the National Assembly is the highest organ of state power, combines the legislative and the executive activities of the State, and exercises supreme control. The National Assembly consists of 400 Deputies each representing constituencies of equal size and elected by universal, direct, equal and secret ballot by all citizens over 18 years. Candidates may stand at 18. It is usual for one approved candidate only to stand for each seat. The National Assembly elects a Chairman and 3 Vice-Chairmen. It also appoints standing commissions to report on Bills and other matters referred to them.

The normal term of office of the National Assembly is 5 years. Elections must be held within 3 months of the expiry of the mandate of the previous National Assembly. The National Assembly may dissolve itself earlier, or prolong itself later, than its normal term, if it deems exceptional circumstances warrant it.

The National Assembly elects and may dismiss the State Council and the Council of Ministers, i.e. the Government. The State Council consists of a Chairman, 2 First Vice-Chairmen, 2 Vice-Chairmen, a Secretary and 17 Members. As the highest organ of the National Assembly, it also combines legislative with executive functions. It is elected from among the Deputies of the National Assembly at the first session of the Assembly by a majority of more than half the total number of Deputies. It retains its powers until a new State Council is elected by a new National Assembly. It is responsible to the National Assembly for all its activities.

The State Council convenes the National Assembly for at least 3 brief, regular sessions a year. It determines the date of general elections, may appoint or dismiss Ministers provided the decision is approved at the next National Assembly sitting, and issues decrees and other juridical acts, either on fundamental questions arising from the laws of the National Assembly, or on matters of principle, or, in cases of emergency, amending individual provisions of laws.

Bills may be proposed by the State Council, the Government, the Deputies of the National Assembly, the Supreme Court or the Chief Prosecutor. In matters affecting themselves certain public organisations may also propose Bills; the Fatherland Front, the trade union organisation, the Young Communist League and the Central Co-operative Committee.

The quorum of the National Assembly is one-half of the Deputies plus 1. Bills are passed into law on a simple majority vote of Deputies present. Sessions are normally public. Laws, when passed, are published in the State Gazette (*Normativni aktove*).

BURMA

In 1962 Burma became a parliamentary democracy, having 2 Houses, the Chamber of Deputies and the Chamber of Nationalities. The latter comprised 125 Members, 62 of whom represented the central unit, 63 the states and special areas. The Chamber of Deputies had twice as many Members. Both were elected for a 4-year term. The Head of State was the President, elected for a 5-year term by both Chambers of Parliament in joint session.

In 1958 Gen. Ne Win, the Army Chief-of-Staff, became Prime Minister of a caretaker government. The elections to the Lower House, held in 1960, gave the Pyidaungsu (Union) Party, led by U Nu, 161 out of 250 seats. In 1962 Gen. Ne Win overthrew the government of U Nu and replaced it by a Revolutionary Council. Parliament and the state councils were dissolved; the latter were reformed as 'state supreme councils' under appointed chairmen. Laws are promulgated by U Ne Win in his own name. His executive functions were normally exercised through the Council of Ministers, usually called the

Government of the Union of Burma.

A new Constitution, under which Burma became a Socialist Republic with a one-party system and an elected unicameral People's National Congress was established in March, 1974. U Ne Win became the first President of the 'Socialist Republic of Burma'.

BURUNDI

Burundi is a Republic and a one-party (*Uprona*) State. A new Constitution was promulgated by the President in July 1974. The President, whose term of office is 7 years, governs through a Council of Ministers and the Political Bureau of the Party. Legislative power rests with the President.

CAMEROUN

Under the Constitution of 1961 the Federal Republic of Cameroun is composed of 1 federal state and 2 federated states, namely East and West Cameroun.

The Executive Head of the Federal Government is the President. He is assisted by a Vice-President who may not belong to the same state as the President. They are elected for a 5-year term by direct and secret, universal adult (at 21 years) suffrage. They can be re-elected.

Legislative power is held by the Federal National Assembly, whose Members are elected for a 5-year term by direct and secret universal adult suffrage. There are 50 Members in the Federal National Assembly, 40 from

East Cameroun and 10 from West Cameroun. The National Assembly shares with the President the initiative for proposing Bills which the Assembly adopts on a simple majority basis. The Assembly adopts the budget and holds 2 ordinary sessions yearly lasting not more than 30 days. The execution of the laws passed by the Assembly is assured by the Government. The Assembly holds public sessions but can also hold private sessions on the request of the Government or of a majority of Members in the House.

CANADA

The federal legislative authority is vested in the Parliament of Canada consisting of the Queen, an Upper House (the Senate), and the House of Commons. Bills may originate in either the Senate or the House, subject to the provisions of Sect. 53 of the British North America Act, 1867, which provides that Bills for the appropriation of any part of the public revenue or the imposition of any tax or impost shall originate in the House of Commons. Bills must pass both Houses and receive Royal Assent before becoming law. In practice, most public Bills originate in the House of Commons, although there has been a marked increase recently in the introduction of public Bills in the Senate, at the instance of the Government, in order that Bills may be dealt with in the Senate while the Commons is engaged in other matters such as the debate on the Speech from the Throne. Private Bills usually originate in the Senate. The Senate may delay, amend or even refuse to pass Bills sent to it from the Commons, but differences are usually settled without serious conflict.

Under Sect. 91 of the British North America Acts, 1867 and 1964, the legislative authority of the Parliament of Canada extends to the following: the amendment of the Constitution of Canada (subject to certain exceptions); the public debt and property; the regulation of trade and commerce; unemployment insurance; the raising of money by any mode or system of taxation; the borrowing of money on the public credit; postal service; the census and statistics; militia, military and naval service, and defence; the fixing of and providing for the salaries and allowances of civil and other officers of the Government of Canada; beacons, buoys, lighthouses and Sable Island; navigation and shipping; quarantine and the establishment and maintenance of marine hospitals; sea coast and inland fisheries; ferries between a province and any British or foreign country or between two provinces; currency and coinage, banking, incorporation of banks and the issue of paper money; savings banks; weights and measures; bills of exchange and promissory notes; interest; legal tender; bankruptcy and insolvency; patents of invention and discovery; copyrights; Indians and lands reserved for the Indians; naturalisation and aliens; marriage and divorce; the criminal law, except the constitution of courts of criminal jurisdiction, but including the procedure in criminal matters; the establishment, maintenance and management of penitentiaries; such classes of subjects as are expressly excepted in the enumeration of the classes of subjects by these Acts assigned exclusively to the legislatures of the provinces.

Under Sect. 95, the Parliament of Canada may make laws in relation to agriculture and immigration concurrently with provincial legislatures although federal legislation is paramount in the event of conflict. By the British North America Act, 1951 (Br. Stat. 1950–1, c. 32), it is declared that the Parliament of Canada may make laws in relation to old-age pensions in Canada, but no such law shall affect·the operation of any provincial laws in relation to old-age pensions. By the British North America Act, 1964, which received Royal Assent on 31 July 1964, this amendment was extended at the request of the Parliament of Canada (19 June 1964) to permit the payment of supplementary benefits, including survivors' and disability benefits irrespective of age, under a contributory pension plan.

From an original membership of 72 at Confederation, the Senate, through the addition of new provinces and the general growth of population, now has 102 Members, the latest change in representation having been made on the admission of Newfoundland to Confederation in 1949.

Senators are appointed by the Governor-General by instrument under the Great Seal of Canada. The actual power of appointing Senators resides by constitutional usage in the Prime Minister, whose advice the Governor-General accepts in this regard. Until the passage of 'An Act to make provision for the retirement of members of the Senate' (SC 1965, c. 4), assented to on 2 June 1965, Senators were appointed for life; that Act fixes at 75 years the age at which any person appointed to the Senate, after the coming into force of the Bill, will cease to hold his place in the Senate.

In each of the four main divisions of Canada, except Quebec, Senators represent the whole of the province for which they are appointed; in Quebec, one Senator is appointed for each of the 24 electoral divisions of what was formerly Lower Canada. The deliberations of the Senate are presided over by a Speaker appointed by the Governor-General in Council (in effect by the Government), and government business in the Senate is sponsored by the Government Leader in the Senate.

The powers of the Senate, in all respects except one, are co-extensive with those of the House of Commons. The one exception is that under the Canadian Constitution all 'money Bills', i.e., Bills to impose taxes or appropriate public moneys, must originate in the House of Commons. The concurrence of the Senate is necessary before any piece of legislation, public or private, can become law. Government Bills, other than money Bills, may be introduced in either House. A substantial pei ·entage of these are now introduced in the Senate where they may be freely discussed and amended and the House of Commons thus given the benefit of their prior scrutiny by the Senate.

The Senate also retains its traditional role in respect of legislation originating in the House of Commons, namely, to take 'a sober second look' at such legislation. Amendments may be made thereto and such amendments are often concurred in by the House of Commons. If there is disagreement concerning such amendments and the disagreement is not resolved by a conference between representatives of the two Houses, the legislation cannot be further proceeded with.

The Senate provides a national forum for the discussion of public issues and the airing of grievances from whatever part of Canada they may emanate. The Senate, through its own committees and its participation in joint committees of both Houses, is particularly active in making studies in depth on matters of public concern.

The British North America Act, 1867, provided that in respect of representation in the House of Commons the province of Quebec should have the fixed number of 65 Members, and that there should be assigned to each of the other provinces such a number of Members as would bear the same proportion to the number of its population as the number 65 bears to the number of the population of Quebec. This Act also provided that on the completion of a census in 1871, and of each subsequent decennial census, the representation of the several provinces should be readjusted, provided the proportional representation of the provinces as prescribed by the Act were not thereby disturbed.

In the session of 1946, the House of Commons adopted a resolution stating that the effect of the provisions of the British North America Act relating to representation had not been satisfactory in that proportionate representation of the provinces according to population had not been maintained, and that a more equitable apportionment of members to the various provinces could be effected if readjustments were made on the basis of the population of all the provinces taken as a whole. The Act was amended accordingly in 1946 to provide a new rule to regulate representation in the House of Commons.

If a Bill is introduced in the House of Commons and is approved there, it must then be introduced into the Senate and follow a procedure similar to that followed in the House. If a Bill is first introduced into the Senate, the reverse procedure is followed. There are three types of Bills: (1) public Bills introduced by the Government; (2) public Bills introduced by private Members of Parliament; and (3) private Bills introduced by private Members of Parliament. Each type is treated in a slightly different manner, and there are even differences in procedure when the House deals with Government Bills introduced pursuant to 'supply' and 'ways and means' motions on the one hand, and other Government Bills on the other. The following is the procedure for a typical Government Bill which has been introduced in the House of Commons.

The sponsoring Minister gives notice that he intends to introduce a Bill on a given subject. Not less than 48 hours later he moves for leave to introduce the Bill and that the Bill be given first reading. This is permitted automatically because introduction or first reading of a Bill does not imply approval of any sort, and it is only after first reading that the Bill is ordered to be printed for distribution to the Members.

At a later sitting, the Minister moves that the Bill be given second reading and that it be referred to an appropriate committee of the House of Commons. A favourable vote on the motion for second reading represents approval of the principle of the Bill, so there is often an extensive debate, which, according to the Standing Orders of the House of Commons, must be confined to the principle of the Bill. The debate culminates in a vote which, if favourable, results in the Bill being referred to the appropriate committee of the House, where it is given clause-by-clause consideration.

At the committee stage, expert witnesses and interested parties may be invited to give testimony pertaining to the Bill, and the proceedings of the committee may cover many weeks. Upon completion of its consideration of the Bill, the House committee prepares a report which it submits to the House of Commons. The House must then decide whether to accept the committee's report, including any amendments that the committee has made to the Bill.

At the report stage any Member may, on giving 24 hours notice, move an amendment to the Bill, and all such amendments are debated and put to a vote. Following that, a motion 'that the bill be concurred in' or 'that the bill, as amended, be concurred in', is put to the vote.

Following this report stage, the Minister moves that the Bill be given third reading and passage. Debate of this motion is limited to whether the Bill should be given third reading. Amendments are permitted at this stage but they must be of a general nature, similar to those allowed on second reading. If the vote is favourable, the Bill is then introduced into the Senate, where it goes through a somewhat similar process. (Since each House has its own rules of procedure, the processes in the two may not be identical, and are not identical at this time.) At the end of this procedure the Bill is presented to the Governor-General for Royal Assent and for his signature. Depending on the provisions in the Bill itself, it may come into force when it is signed by the Governor-General on an appointed day, or when it is officially proclaimed.

PROVINCIAL LEGISLATURES

The source of legislative authority for each province and territory is the British North America Act, 1867. This lays down limits of provincial authority.

Provinces may make laws to amend their Constitutions, except for anything affecting the position of the Lieutenant-Governor; provincial taxation; borrowing money on the province's credit; provincial offices; public lands in the province; prisons, hospitals, asylums, charities etc., in the province;

municipal institutions and local works; licences to raise provincial revenue; company incorporation; marriage, property, civil rights in the province; administration of justice in the province.

Provinces may also legislate for education in the province, subject to certain restrictions regarding schools for religious minorities. They may also legislate for agriculture and immigration, provided that such legislation does not clash with any laws of the Parliament of Canada.

In each province the legislature is unicameral. It may be dissolved by the Lieutenant-Governor on the advice of the Premier within its usual 5-year term. The relationship between the Queen, the Lieutenant-Governor and the provincial House is the same as that between the Queen, the Governor-General and the Canadian Parliament.

Bills may originate anywhere in the Houses, except for major finance Bills which only come from Ministers. Discussion in party group before presentation is carried out. There are 3 readings. The first to introduce, the second discussion in principle followed by committee examination, the third for passing or rejecting the amended Bill. If passed, it goes to the Lieutenant-Governor for assent, which he gives on the advice of the Premier.

This process is universal in Canadian provinces, none of which have an Upper House. In very small Houses (e.g. Prince Edward Island) 'committee' discussion tends to be replaced by session because the whole House is only the size of a committee anyway.

Alberta

Alberta formed part of Rupert's Land until it became a province in 1905. The Constitution provides for a single Chamber which is the Legislative Assembly. There are 75 members elected for a 5-year term by universal suffrage at 18 years. All Members have to be qualified as electors.

British Columbia

British Columbia became a crown colony in 1858, and the present Constitution dates from its becoming a province in 1871. A single Chamber is provided in which there are 55 Members elected for a 5-year term by universal suffrage at 19 years. All Members have to be qualified as electors.

Manitoba

Manitoba was originally the Red River Settlement with no responsible government, and became a dominion in 1870 with a Constitution providing a single Chamber. The Legislative Assembly has 57 Members elected for a 5-year term by universal suffrage at 18 years. All Members have to be qualified as electors. Women were enfranchised in 1916.

New Brunswick

Responsible government was instituted in 1848 with a Constitution providing an Executive Council, a Legislative Council (which was later abolished), and a House of Assembly. The first party government took office in 1854. There are 58 Members elected for a 5-year term by universal suffrage at 21 years. Candidates must be qualified electors over 21 years.

Newfoundland

The legislature was first introduced in 1832, but the Governor and his Executive were not responsible to it. In 1855 a Constitution was introduced providing a House of Assembly of 27 elected Members (on a property franchise) and a Legislative Council of 24 Members nominated by the Governor. The Governor and his Executive are responsible to the 2 Houses. Newfoundland achieved Dominion status in 1917. Women were enfranchised in 1925. A financial crisis, in which the Dominion could not support its own administration, arose in 1934, and a Government by Commission was inaugurated on 16 Feb. 1934.

In 1948 there were 2 referenda on possible future forms of government. The first was indecisive, but the second favoured a union with Canada, which was effected in Nov. 1948. The Constitution continued as it had been prior to 1934, subject to authority of various British North America Acts, except that the Legislative Council was not continued. Newfoundland may, at any time, re-establish it or establish a new one. There are 42 Members elected for a 5-year term by universal suffrage at 19 years, with usual residence qualifications. All who qualify as electors also qualify to be elected. Direct election takes place from single-member constituencies.

Northwest Territories

The Northwest Territories Act of 1875 established a non-responsible government and in 1905 provision was made for a federally appointed Commissioner and an appointed Council of 4 Members, which in 1921 was extended to 6. In 1952 the number of Members went up to 8, 3 of whom were elected. Council sessions have to be held twice a year at least—once in the territories and, at all other times, at Federal Government in Ottawa. The subjects for legislation are roughly the same as for Yukon, i.e. do not include natural resources.

In 1966 electoral representation was introduced for all inhabitants, including Eskimos, and in 1970 there was a federal amendment to the Northwest Territories Act which extended the number of Council Members to 14, 10 of whom are elected. Members sit for a 4-year term.

The Commissioner obtains federal approval for all measures before submitting them to the Council. He is appointed by Federal Government but, in practice, he takes all major decisions on the Council's advice; he may only spend according to funds voted by the Council.

Private Members' Bills may be introduced, but financial measures are the prerogative of the Commissioner.

Nova Scotia

The history of the legislature of Nova Scotia dates from 1791 when a Legislative Council was instituted which was nominated by the Governor for life, and a Legislative Assembly was elected on a property franchise. The Governor and his Executive were not responsible to them and could overrule them. In the years 1840 and 1848, there were votes of 'no confidence' in the Legislative Council passed by the Assembly, which led to the first party government taking office in 1951.

There are 46 Members elected for 5 years by universal suffrage at 19 years, with usual residence qualifications. Candidates must be qualified as electors, British subjects or Canadian citizens of at least 19 years.

Ontario

The Canada Act, 1791, provided a Legislative Council nominated for life and an Assembly elected on a property franchise; the Crown reserved the right to disallow laws passed and the Governor was responsible only to the British Government. As in Quebec, there were long, drawn-out conflicts between the elected Assembly and the Legislative Council and Governor. The Legislative Assembly was dissolved after refusing to vote supplies in 1836, and armed rebellion broke out the following year. As a result of investigations following this, Lord Durham advocated union, which was effected in 1840. (*See* Quebec.)

Confederation took place in 1867 and a Constitution was set up with a one-chamber legislature, which is the House of Assembly. There are 117 Members elected for a 5-year term by universal suffrage at 18 years. All Members have to be qualified as electors.

Prince Edward Island

A legislature was summoned in 1773, but the Executive was not responsible to it. It took the form of a nominated Legislative Council and a Legislative Assembly elected on a property franchise. In 1839 the Legislative Council was separated from the Executive and in 1851 a responsible government was established. In 1893 a Legislature Act formed the present House and abolished the existing two Houses.

There are 32 Members elected for a 5-year term by universal suffrage at 18 years, with residence qualification. There are 2 Members for each district; one is called an Assemblyman and the other, a Councillor. All Members must be British subjects or Canadian citizens over 21 years.

Quebec

The Canada Act of 1791 set up a Legislative Assembly elected on property franchise, and a nominated Legislative Council. The Governor and the Legislative Council could overrule and were not responsible to the Legislative Assembly.

In 1837 the Constitution was suspended after a rebellion, and in 1840 an Act of Union united Lower Canada (Quebec) with Upper (Ontario) to share a legislature with a Legislative Council of at least 20 life Members and a Legislative Assembly of 84 elected Members. After Confederation in 1867 Quebec retained a bicameral legislature. The Legislative Council, which was non-elective, was abolished in 1968.

The National Assembly (now only one House) has 108 Members elected for a 5-year term in single-member constituencies by universal suffrage at 18 years. All Members have to be qualified as electors.

Saskatchewan

Saskatchewan originally formed part of the Northwest Territories with no responsible government, and became a province in 1905 with a Constitution providing a single Chamber. Women were enfranchised in 1916.

There are 59 Members elected for a 5-year term by universal suffrage at 18 years. All Members have to be qualified as electors.

Yukon Territory

The Yukon Territory was made a separate territory in 1898, with a Commissioner and an appointed Legislative Council of 6 Members. The

Commissioner in Council had legislative power. In 1908 the Council became fully elective and the membership was extended to 10, the population having risen after the gold rush. In 1919 the Council was reduced to 3 Members in the population decline. By 1960, however, the population had risen again and the Council was increased to 7 Members elected by universal suffrage. The Council is representative but not responsible, and its authority does not come from the British North America Act, but only by federal legislation. It does not extend to legislating about natural resources, which are managed by the federal Department of Indian Affairs and Northern Development.

Bills have 3 readings as elsewhere, and the committee discussion is usually by Committee of the Whole hearing expert advice.

CAYMAN ISLANDS

The Legislative Assembly is comprised of 12 elected Members and 3 official Members with the Governor as President. Provision is made in the Constitution for the appointment of a Speaker, if deemed desirable, and the House has a 4-year term.

The voting age is 18 years, and in order to be placed on the Electoral Roll a person must be a British subject who has been resident in the islands for at least 5 years out of the 7 prior to registration. Candidates must be over 21 years, have resided in the islands for 5 out of the 7 years immediately preceding the date of nomination, or have been born in the islands or be domiciled in the islands at the date of nomination.

CENTRAL AFRICAN REPUBLIC

On 1 Jan. 1966 the army overthrew the government. The Constitution was rescinded and the National Assembly was dissolved. On 4 Jan. 1966 an Act was adopted giving the President full competence to act in all affairs of state.

CHAD

The President holds the executive power and is assisted by a Council of Ministers. Ministers are appointed by the President. Legislation is carried out by the Legislative Assembly of 105 Members elected by universal direct suffrage for a 5-year term. Chad has been a one-party state since Nov. 1965.

CHANNEL ISLANDS

For the purposes of government and the administration of justice, the Channel Islands comprise two quite distinct Bailiwicks, i.e. those of Guernsey and Jersey. The Bailiwick of Guernsey consists of Guernsey, (including Herm and Jethou), Alderney and Sark. Although the Guernsey legislature and courts have certain powers and jurisdiction in relation to Alderney and Sark, both of the latter have their own legislatures and courts.

Guernsey

The States, as a legislative and deliberative assembly, came into being in the fifteenth and sixteenth centuries, and although it gained importance over the years, particularly during the nineteenth century, it was not until the 1948 reforms that the Royal Court surrendered to the States the last of its legislative functions.

The island's legislature is the States of Deliberation. It is composed of three different groups of people, the three groups being elected differently but with each Member having one vote. The modern States consist of:

The Bailiff who is appointed by Royal Warrant and is the civil head of the island. He presides over the States in which he has a voice and a casting vote, and lays before the States such matters as he is requested so to do by the various States Committees. He is also President of the Royal Court and as such is, in modern times, invariably a lawyer.

The origins of the appointment of Bailiff are a little obscure, but he was probably originally appointed and paid by the Warden. (The Wardens were usually fairly important men at the English Court, or soldiers, and they were frequently absent from the islands for very long periods and appointed Bailiffs to act for them. Gradually the Bailiff acquired an independent position and in the early part of the fourteenth century the office of Bailiff was established in its own right and recognised as such by the Crown.)

The 12 Conseillers, who are elected by the States of Election. The latter is an electoral college which consists of the Bailiff, the 12 Jurats, the 12 Conseillers, the 10 rectors of the parishes, the Law Officers (i.e. H M Attorney-General and H M Solicitor-General), 33 People's Deputies, 34 Douzaine representatives and 4 representatives of the States of Alderney.

The Conseillers are usually chosen from people who have served the island for a considerable time as States Members or in one of the important parochial offices. They hold office for 6 years, 6 retiring every 3 years. They do not sit separately in the States and have no special powers of any kind but, because of their standing as 'elder statesmen', the Conseillers as a body do exercise a restraining and stabilising influence, and help to maintain continuity.

The 33 People's Deputies who are elected triennially on a parochial basis by adult suffrage.

The Douzaine, or Parish Council, of each of the 10 parishes, who elect a representative annually to sit in the States. These Representatives are required to voice the opinion of their Douzaines in the States, but are free to vote according to their own conscience.

H M Procureur (Attorney-General) *and H M Comptroller* (Solicitor-General), who are both appointed by Royal Warrant, sit *ex-officio* and have a voice but no vote.

Two Alderney Members of the States, who are appointed by the States of Alderney in view of the fact that Guernsey can legislate for Alderney on certain matters. These Alderney members are full members of the States of Guernsey and may speak and vote on any matter.

The States initiate two forms of legislation, namely Orders in Council and Ordinances.

An Order in Council originates by the passing by the States of a Bill, or *Projet de Loi,* which is designed to implement proposals laid before it by one or more of the States Committees. This Bill has no force of law until, having been transmitted by the Lieutenant-Governor to the Sovereign in Council, it has received the Sovereign's Sanction. This Royal Sanction, which ratifies the Bill, is contained in an Order in Council, which is transmitted to the Royal Court through the Lieutenant-Governor and which directs that it, and the Law with it, be registered on the records of the island.

Ordinances, which also implement States Resolutions, come into force without reference to the Crown. Ordinances, broadly speaking, deal with only relatively minot matters. Some Laws specifically contain the power for certain things in them to be effected by Ordinance.

The States of Guernsey may also legislate on any matter for Alderney and Sark, with the consent of the States of Alderney and the Chief Pleas of Sark respectively. It may also legislate on criminal matters for Alderney and Sark without their consent and also, in the case of Alderney, without their consent as regards adoption, the airfield, education, health services, immigration, police and social services.

Some Acts of Parliament in which the Islands are named apply here as law after being transmitted for registration by way of an Order in Council and registered by the Royal Court. The usual practice of today is for an Act of Parliament, which is to apply to the Bailiwick, to contain a provision enabling it to be extended by Order in Council with such exceptions, modifications and adaptations as may be necessary.

The government of the island is performed not by a Cabinet or Government but by the States through its many States Committees. There are no party politics in the States.

Alderney

The insular legislature of Alderney, the States of Alderney, consists of the President, who is directly elected by popular vote for a 3-year term and who has a voice and a casting vote, and 12 Members of the States, who hold office for a 3-year term. It has in Alderney the same power of legislating as the States of Guernsey has in Guernsey, but legislation in certain matters is reserved to the States of Guernsey. The States nominates 2 of their members to represent Alderney in the Guernsey States of Deliberations and 4 in the Guernsey States of Election. There is universal adult suffrage and the adult age is 20 years.

As in Guernsey, a Law originates in the passing by the States of a *Projet de Loi* or Bill drafted in implementation of proposals laid before them by one or another of their Committees. The *Projet de Loi* becomes Law when it receives the sanction of the Sovereign contained in an Order in Council, which is then, together with the Law accompanying it, entered in the Register of the Island of Guernsey, and observed accordingly.

The States exercise legislative power by way of Ordinance which is limited in scope and, in particular, cannot impose taxation or involve the expenditure of public funds, or alter a Law or the Common Law.

Sark

The insular legislature of Sark, the Chief Pleas, consists of the Seigneur or Dame, who holds the Seigneurie and Fief of Sark directly from the Sovereign, the Seneschal, appointed by the Lieutenant-Governor on the recommendation of the Seigneur or Dame for a 3-year term, the 'Tenants', of whom there are 40 by virtue of the original Charter granted by Elizabeth I, and 12 elected People's Deputies who hold office for a 3-year term. It has the same power of legislating as do the States of Guernsey, subject to the limitations mentioned above. The officials of the Chief Pleas are all nominated by the Seigneur. They are the Seneschal, the Greffier and the Prévôt. There are 2 constables elected annually by the Chief Pleas. The Chief Pleas can only be held in the presence of the Seigneur or his accredited deputy. There is universal adult suffrage at 20 years.

Jersey

The island legislature is 'The States of Jersey', the name being derived from the estates of the realm, originally the judiciary, the clergy and the people.

In the fifteenth century rivalry sprang up between the Royal Court and the States as to the making of laws, and it was only in 1771 that the functions of these two bodies were defined, the States to become a Legislative

Assembly while the Royal Court to administer judgements on breaches of the laws. A result of the passing of the Reform Bill in the United Kingdom (1832) was that in 1856 the Deputies elected by the people were admitted to the States, for up to that date the only Members elected by popular suffrage were the Jurats and Connétables. There were two anomalies in the Constitution of the States. Firstly, the Jurats who helped to make the laws tried persons who had disobeyed them; and secondly, the Rectors who were nominated by the Crown were not popularly elected. This became apparent during the Occupation and agitations resulted in a Referendum being taken in 1947 on the subject of the Reform of the States, 64 per cent of the electorate was in favour and 36 per cent against. In 1948 the States passed their Reform Bill.

The States comprise the Bailiff, the Lieutenant-Governor, 12 Senators, the Constables of the 12 parishes of the island, 28 Deputies, the Dean of Jersey, the Attorney-General and the Solicitor-General. They all have the right to speak in the Assembly, but only the 52 elected Members (the Senators, Constables and Deputies) have the right to vote; the Bailiff has a casting vote.

Senators are elected by the electors of the whole island for a 6-year term, 6 retiring in every third year.

The Constables are Members of the States by virtue of their office, to which they are elected for a 3-year term by the electors of the parish. If unable to attend a sitting of the States, they are represented by the next senior officer of their parish.

Deputies are elected on a constituency basis for a 3-year term.

General elections for Senators and Deputies are held in every third year, the election for Senators being held in the month of Nov. and the election for Deputies being held in the month of Dec.

Except in specific instances, enactments passed by the States require the sanction of H M Elizabeth II in Council.

The administration of the island's affairs is carried out by Committees of the States, which in many instances have powers very similar to those of Ministers in the United Kingdom Government.

CHILE

By the Constitution of 1925, legislative power is vested in the National Congress, consisting of the Senate and the Chamber of Deputies, both of which are elected by direct popular vote. The Senate consists of 50 Members, elected for 8 years, who represent 10 provincial groups, each of which elects 5 Senators. One-half of the Senate is renewable every 4 years. The Chamber of Deputies consists of Members elected for a 4-year term by departments or groups of departments, 1 Member for every 30,000 inhabitants or fraction over 15,000. There was a system of proportional representation. Electors are all citizens of 18 years or over. Women were enfranchised in 1949. Congress sits from 21 May (Navy Day) to 18 Sept. (Independence Day), excluding extraordinary sessions.

The President is elected for a 6-year term, by direct popular vote, but is not eligible for re-election; he must be Chilean-born and over 30 years of age. Normally there is no Vice-President, but the President may appoint one temporarily, usually the Minister of the Interior, when ill or out of the country. He has a modified veto; a Bill which he has vetoed may, by a two-thirds vote of the Members of both Chambers (a majority of the Members being present), be sustained and become law.

The validity of all elections of President, Deputies and Senators is determined by a special body called *Tribunal Calificador,* consisting of 5 Members chosen by lot from past Presidents or Vice-Presidents of the Chamber and Senate, Members of the Supreme Court, of the Court of Appeal of the city where Congress meets.

A military junta assumed power on 11 Sept. 1973 and on 13 Sept. Congress was dissolved and all seats declared vacant. A Commission was then appointed to draft a new Constitution.

PEOPLE'S REPUBLIC OF CHINA

The National People's Congress is the highest organ of state power and the sole legislative authority. It can amend the Constitution, elects and has power to remove from office the highest state dignitaries, decides on the national economic plan and on questions of war and peace, etc. The Congress elects a Standing Committee which conducts the elections, convenes Congress, interprets laws, adopts decrees, supervises the work of government, etc.

The Constitution provides that the Congress be elected for a 4-year term and should meet at least once a year. It is composed of Deputies elected by provinces, autonomous regions, municipalities directly administered by the Government, the armed forces and Chinese resident abroad. According to the Electoral Law as amended in 1963, the provinces and autonomous regions elect 1 Deputy for every 400,000 persons (or 10 Deputies from each province, whichever be the greater); government-administered cities, industrial cities and industrial districts with populations of 200,000–300,000 elect 1 Deputy for every 50,000 persons; the national minorities, 300 Deputies; the armed forces, 120 Deputies; the overseas Chinese, 30 Deputies ('to be elected from among returned overseas Chinese'). The Third Congress, elected in Sept. 1964, consists of 3,040 Deputies, compared with 1,226 before the revision of the electoral law. It has met only once, in Dec. 1964–Jan. 1965. The Fourth Congress has yet to be elected.

The State Council is the executive organ of the Congress, that is, the Central People's Government. It consists of the Premier, several Vice-Premiers, Ministers and Heads of Commissions. It issues directives, and, *inter alia,* supervises the work of Ministries, Commissions and local government authorities, administers the national economic plan and supervises the direction of foreign affairs and foreign trade.

COLOMBIA

The legislative power rests with a Congress (*Congreso*) of 2 Houses, the Senate (*Senado*) of 112 Members and the House of Representatives (*Cámara de Representantes*) of 199 Members, both elected for a 4-year term. In 1968 a congressional committee unanimously approved a constitutional amendment providing that there must be 2 Senators for every Department and one more for each 200,000 inhabitants. It also provides that there will be 2 Representatives for every department and one more for each 100,000 inhabitants. Congress meets annually at Bogotá on 20 July. Women were enfranchised on 25 Aug. 1954 and election is by universal suffrage at 21 years.

The President is elected by direct vote of the people for a 4-year term, and is not eligible for re-election until 4 years has elapsed. Congress elects, for a 2-year term, 1 substitute to occupy the Presidency in the event of a vacancy during a presidential term. There are 13 Ministries. The Governors of Departments and the Mayor of Bogotá are nominated by the National Government.

CONGO

The Congolese Workers' Party is the source of political authority in the People's Republic. The President of its central committee and the Chairman of its political bureau is the President of the Republic. The President is elected for a 5-year term and is also Head of State. The National Assembly was dissolved in 1968. A new Constitution was adopted in 1972 which provided for a Prime Minister and a National Assembly. There are 115 Members of the Assembly who are elected by universal adult (18 years) suffrage.

COSTA RICA

The legislative power is normally vested in a single Chamber called the Legislative Assembly (*Asamblea Legislativa*), which, since 1962, consists of 57 Deputies, 1 for every 25,214 inhabitants, elected for a 4-year term. The President is elected for a 4-year term; the candidate receiving the largest vote, provided it is over 40 per cent of the total, is declared elected, but a second ballot is required if no candidate gets 40 per cent of the total. By the election law of 1946, all citizens who are 20 years are entitled to vote; married men and teachers, from 18 years. Women over 21 were enfranchised in 1949. Elections are normally held on the first Sunday in February. Voting for President, Deputies and municipal councillors is secret and compulsory for all men under 70 years of age. Independent non-Party candidates are barred from the ballot.

The Constitution forbids the establishment or maintenance of an army.

CUBA

From 1 Jan. 1959 the government has been administered under the Fundamental Law of the Republic of Cuba when the bicameral Congress (*Congreso*) was abolished. The Prime Minister appoints the President who governs the Republic, aided by an Executive Committee and various Ministers. The country is divided into 6 provinces and 126 municipalities. No elections have been held since 1959.

CYPRUS

The legislative power is exercised by the House of Representatives (*Vouli Antiprosópon-Temsilciler Meclisi*) of 50 Members, of whom 35 were elected by the Greek community and 15 by the Turkish community. From Dec. 1963 the Turkish members have ceased to attend.

CZECHOSLOVAKIA

Czechoslovakia is a Federal State of two nations of equal rights: the Czech Socialist Republic and the Slovak Republic. The national legislature is the Federal Assembly (*Federální Shromáždění*) consisting of two Chambers, the House of the People (*Snemovna Lidu*) and the House of the Nations (*Snêmovna Narodů*). The two Houses have equal rights. The House of the People is composed of 200 Deputies representing equal constituencies on a. purely demographic basis: in 1974 there were 137 Czech constituencies and 63 Slovak. For the House of the Nations of 150 Deputies, 75 constituencies are allotted to the Czech Lands, and 75 to Slovakia, regardless of the number of residents. Deputies to both Houses are elected for a 5-year term by universal, direct, equal and secret elections. Citizens may vote at 18 and stand as candidates at 21. All candidates must belong to the National Front. It is usual for one candidate only to stand in each constituency.

The Czech Lands and Slovakia both have their own legislatures in the National Councils (*Národní Rada*). Federal Government portfolios have their cognates in the national governments, but only the Federal Government is competent in the sphere of defence, foreign relations, foreign trade and transport.

The outgoing Presidium of the Federal Assembly must convene both Houses of the newly-elected Federal Assembly not later than 4 weeks after the general election.

Each House elects a Presidium, consisting of a Chairman, a Vice-Chairman and from 3 to 6 Members. Both Houses elect the Presidium of the Federal Assembly, consisting of 40 Members, 20 elected by the House of the

People, and 20 by the House of the Nations. The latter elects 10 Czechs and 10 Slovaks. The Federal Assembly also elects a Chairman and a Vice-Chairman from among the Presidium. If the Chairman is a Czech, the Vice-Chairman must be a Slovak, and vice versa.

Sessions of each House are convened by the Presidium of the House, or at the request of at least one-third of the Deputies giving at least 30 days' notice.

Joint sessions of both Houses are convened for the election of the President of Czechoslovakia, for the election of the Chairman and Vice-Chairman of the Federal Assembly Presidium, and for the discussion of 'programmatic proposals' of the Government. They may also be convened if deemed necessary by the Federal Assembly Presidium, or upon the resolution of both Houses.

The quorum in the House of the People is one-half of all Deputies plus 1; in the House of the Nations it is one-half plus 1 of all the Czech Deputies and one-half plus 1 of all the Slovak. Sessions of both Houses are normally public.

Regular sessions of the Federal Assembly are held twice a year, in spring and autumn. Between sessions, the Federal Assembly Presidium carries on the business of the Assembly, submitting its enactments for approval at the next Federal Assembly sitting.

The Presidium of one House must keep informed the Presidia of the other House and of the Federal Assembly, of all decisions taken by its House. If the Houses cannot agree, they must elect Joint Committees consisting of 10 Members from each House. The 10 Members from the House of the Nations must be 5 Czechs and 5 Slovaks. If these Joint Committees cannot reach agreement, the President of Czechoslovakia must be informed. Deputies have the right to interpellate Ministers.

Bills may be proposed by individual Deputies, groups of Deputies, committees of either House, the President of Czechoslovakia, the Czech Government or the Slovak Government. Bills are passed into law in both Houses by the vote of a majority of Deputies present. Bills become law not more than 14 days after their adoption by the Federal Assembly, and are published in the official gazette (*Zbirka zákonů*). In the case of Bills adopted by one House, this day is the day they are voted by the other House. If this does not happen within three months, the Federal Assembly Presidium promulgates the law. Motions to elect the President of Czechoslovakia, declare war or amend the Constitution, require a three-fifths majority in both Houses.

The Czech National Council consists of 200 Deputies, the Slovak of 150. The National Councils are elected for 5 years, sit twice a year, normally in spring and autumn, and in most other respects their structure and procedure follows that of the Federal Assembly closely.

DAHOMEY

A military government rules Dahomey. Since 1973 the National Council of the Revolution of 66 Members has helped to define government policy. The unicameral National Consultative Assembly (*Assemblée Nationale Consultative*) of 45 nominated Members was dissolved in 1972.

DENMARK

The legislative power lies with the Queen and the Diet (*Folketing*) jointly. The executive power is vested in the Queen, who exercises her authority through the Ministers. The Queen must be a member of the Evangelical-Lutheran Church, the official Church of the State. The Queen cannot assume major international obligations without the consent of the *Folketing*. The *Folketing* consists of one Chamber. All men and women of Danish nationality of 20 years and over and permanently resident in Denmark possess the franchise and are eligible for election to the *Folketing*, which is at present composed of 179 Members; 135 Members are elected by the method of proportional representation in 17 districts. In order to attain an equal representation of the different parties, 40 *tillægsmandater* (additional seats) are divided among such parties which have not obtained sufficient returns at the district elections. Two members are elected for the Faroe Islands and 2 for Greenland. The legislature has a 4-year term, but a general election may be called at any time.

The *Folketing* must meet every year on the first Tuesday in October. Besides its legislative functions, it appoints every 6 years judges who, together with the ordinary Members of the Supreme Court (*Højesteret*), form the *Rigsret*, a tribunal which can alone try parliamentary impeachments. The Ministers have free access to the House, but can vote only if they are Members.

Any member may initiate a Bill. Bills are approved or not after 3 readings. If one-third of members request it, a Bill that has been passed may be subject to a referendum. A Bill that is to be subject to referendum may be withdrawn within 5 weeks of its being passed. The referendum is held and its result acted upon in accordance with the Prime Minister's decision.

DOMINICAN REPUBLIC

Legislative power is exercised by Congress which consists of a Senate and Chamber of Deputies. Senators and Deputies are elected for a 4-year term. They must be citizens of the Republic and over 25 years.

Decisions of Congress are taken by absolute majority of at least 50 per cent of each House. Some exceptional Bills require a majority of two-thirds.

A new constitution was promulgated in 1966. The President is elected for a 4-year term, by direct vote. In case of death, resignation or disability, he is succeeded by the Vice-President. There are 12 Secretaries of State, a Judicial Adviser with secretary-of-state rank and 2 Ministers without portfolio in charge of departments. Citizens are entitled to vote at the age of 18 years, or less when married.

ECUADOR

Legislative power is exercised by Congress consisting of a Senate and a Chamber of Deputies. Senators are elected for a 4-year term and Deputies for a 2-year term.

Initiation of laws was in the hands of the legislative departments, but has now been conceded to the executive and to the Supreme Court of Justice. Since 1945, a Permanent Legislative Commission has been created which, during the recess of Congress, takes the place of the latter in drafting certain laws. When a law has been drafted it is sent to the President of the Republic for his sanction or rejection. If sanctioned, it is promulgated. If there is an objection, it is returned to the Chamber of origin within ten days with the appropriate observations whether they refer to unconstitutionality or unacceptability. The objection may be to the entire proposal or constitute mere reforms or modifications. If the President does not return the proposal either sanctioned or with objections within ten days, or if he does not sanction it after the appropriate constitutional steps have been taken, the proposal will become law. The law does not come into force except by virtue of its promulgation which is effected by publication in the *Registro Oficial* (Official Register).

Every citizen who is literate and over 18 years must vote.

ARAB REPUBLIC OF EGYPT

The National Assembly is elected by universal suffrage and has 360 Members; the President of the Republic may appoint up to 10 additional Members. The President of the Republic is nominated by the National Assembly and confirmed by plebiscite for a 6-year term.

In exceptional conditions the National Assembly can authorise the President to rule by decree. This requires a two-third majority and decrees must be approved by the Assembly at its next meeting.

EL SALVADOR

Legislative power is exercised by a unicameral Legislative Assembly of 52 Deputies elected for a 2-year term. Voting is by a system of proportional representation. Executive power is vested in the President, who serves a 5-year term, and is assisted by a Cabinet. There is universal adult suffrage at 18 years.

EQUATORIAL GUINEA

Legislative power rests with the National Assembly. The Assembly consists of 35 Members elected by universal, direct and secret ballot.

The President of the Republic and the Assembly are elected for a 5-year term but the first President was appointed for life on 14 July 1972. There is a Cabinet of 9 Ministers.

ETHIOPIA

Ethiopa was governed by a Council of Ministers, responsible to the Emperor, and a Parliament consisting of a Senate and a Chamber of Deputies. The Chamber of Deputies consists of 250 Members; the number of Senators must not exceed half the number of Deputies.

In 1955 a new Constitution was promulgated and this was revised in 1974. This provided for universal suffrage at 21 years, for greater fiscal control by the Chamber, and for a limited degree of ministerial responsibility to Parliament. The Chambers met in joint session or separately. Bills were presented by either or both Chambers, by the Emperor, or by 10 Members of either Chamber. If an emergency arose during a parliamentary recess the Emperor could promulgate a decree, but this was eventually ratified by Parliament. All financial laws originated in the Chamber of Deputies.

The Emperor was deposed in Sept. 1974. A draft Constitution has been published and this modifies the 1955 Constitution by vesting sovereignty solely in the people and providing for the separation of power between the legislature, the executive and the judiciary.

FALKLAND ISLANDS

The Colony is administered by a Governor, assisted by an Executive Council consisting of the Colonial Secretary and Colonial Treasurer, both *ex officio*; 2 Members elected by the Legislature and 2 appointed Members; and a Legislative Council composed of the Colonial Secretary and Colonial Treasurer, both *ex officio*, 2 elected Members representing Stanley, one elected Member from the East Falkland and one from the West Falkland and 2 nominated independent Members.

FIJI

Fiji became an independent nation with Dominion status within the Commonwealth on 10 Oct. 1970. This had been agreed at a constitutional conference held in London in April 1970. At the first general election for the House of Representatives since independence, held April 1972, the ruling Alliance Party was returned with 33 seats; National Federation Party, 19 seats. The election was held under a system designed to return 22 Fijian, 22 Indian and 8 representatives of other races. There is also an Upper House, the Senate, of 22 Members (8 nominations by the Council of Chiefs, 7 by the Prime Minister, 6 by the Leader of the Opposition and 1 by the Rotuma Council). The maximum term in office is 4 years.

FINLAND

Parliament consists of one Chamber (*Eduskunta-Riksdagen*) of 200 Members chosen by direct and proportional election, by universal suffrage at 18 years. The country is divided into 15 electoral districts with a representation proportional to their population. Every citizen entitled to vote is eligible for Parliament, which is elected for a 4-year term, but can be dissolved sooner by the President. Voting is not compulsory.

Parliament convenes for ordinary session on 1 Feb. each year without special summons, unless another date has been set at the preceding session.

The initiative for matters to be considered by Parliament is taken either by the Government, or by one or more Members of Parliament. Most of the motions presented by the Government are government Bills. Legislative Bills and the budget Bill, amongst others, are introduced in Parliament in this form. The Government may further render an account or give notification to Parliament concerning a matter of public administration or the relations of the country with foreign powers. Such an account must then be dealt with in the order prescribed by the Parliament Act. The reports submitted to Parliament by the Government (on the state of public finance, on the measures taken by the Government upon the resolution of Parliament, and on any other important events concerned with public administration or relations with foreign states), may also lead to the adoption of measures by Parliament.

A Member may bring a matter before Parliament by presenting a written question to a member of the Government, who must give a written or oral reply. But Parliament cannot debate or pass resolutions on an individual question of this kind. Only if 20 Members join in addressing a question or interpellation to a Minister, may there be a debate after the Minister concerned has given an oral reply, or the Government has stated that, owing to the nature of the matter, no reply will be given. Parliament may subsequently pass a resolution on the point raised.

In general, all matters to be treated in plenary session, but not interpellations and certain other questions, are prepared for consideration in committees. If a report by a committee relates to the adoption or rejection of a draft Bill, the matter will be taken up in plenary session.

At the first reading, a debate is allowed; the matter is then remitted, without decision on points of substance, to the Grand Committee.

At the second reading, the report of the Grand Committee is presented, and Parliament proceeds to examine the Bill. If the proposal of the Grand Committee is accepted in every respect, the second reading will be declared concluded. But if the proposal is not accepted without amendments, the Bill will be returned to the Grand Committee, which either agrees to the draft as proposed by Parliament, or makes its own amendments, or proposes the Bill to be rejected. If the Grand Committee has proposed amendments,

Parliament decides upon their adoption or rejection, and the second reading is concluded.

At the third reading, the Bill is presented for final decision. Parliament may either adopt it without amendments, in the form drafted at the second reading, or reject it. Amendments are no longer permitted at the third reading.

However, apart from adopting or rejecting the Bill, Parliament may at this reading also decide to leave the Bill pending until the first session after new elections. This requires the support of one third of all members of Parliament.

The President of the Republic takes part in the legislative process, first by virtue of his right of initiative, i.e. his power to propose that a new law be enacted, or an existing statute be amended, interpreted or anulled. It is the President who decides upon the introduction of government Bills to Parliament. But the co-operation of the President is also needed at the other end of the legislative process. Before a Bill adopted by Parliament becomes an Act, the assent and signature of the President are necessary. He cannot make any amendments to the Bill, and must either give or refuse assent. The President is considered to have refused his assent if he has not accepted the Bill within 3 months of the date when the Bill was submitted to him. But although the President has refused his signature, a Bill may become law, if, after a new election, Parliament passes the Bill without changes by a majority of the votes cast. In such a case the President must sign the Bill. The President may thus only postpone the validation of an Act of Parliament, but cannot block it. He has a suspensive veto.

Under normal circumstances the President is elected for a 6-year term, and is re-eligible. He must be a Finnish citizen by birth. The election is made by a college of 300 presidential electors. These are elected in the same manner as Members of Parliament, i.e. by universal adult suffrage under a system of proportional representation.

FRANCE

The Constitution of the Fifth Republic, superseding that of 1946, came into force on 4 Oct. 1958.

In the Constitution emphasis is placed on the rôle of the President of the Republic. 'He sees that the Constitution is respected; he ensures, through his arbitration, the regular functioning of public powers as well as the continuity of the state. He is the guarantor of national independence.' He nominates and dismisses the Prime Minister and the other members of the Government. He can dissolve the National Assembly after consultation with the Prime Minister and the Presidents of the Assemblies. He appoints to all military and civil offices of the Republic. 'When the institutions of the Republic, the independence of the Nation, the integrity of its territory or the fulfilment of its international commitments are threatened with immediate and grave danger, and when the regular functioning of constitutional public powers is interrupted, the President of the Republic takes the measures demanded by the circumstances, after official consultation with the Prime Minister, the presidents of the assemblies and the Constitutional Council.' Under the revised Article 6 of the Constitution (6 Nov. 1962) the President of the Republic is now elected by direct universal suffrage. His term of office is 7 years.

'The Government determines and conducts the policy of the nation'; 'the government may ask parliament for authority to take, by decrees and within a limited period, such measures as are normally within the province of the law.' Ministers must not be Members of Parliament. Votes of censure can only be carried by a majority of the Members constituting the Assembly. The 2 ordinary sessions in autumn and spring are curtailed to a total of 5 months. The 'Council of the Republic' has been re-named 'Senate'. The 'Economic Council' has been re-named 'Economic and Social Council'. The 'Constitutional Council' has to uphold the fairness of the elections and to act as a guardian of the Constitution. It is composed of 9 Members, 3 of whom are nominated by the President of the Republic, 3 by the President of the National Assembly and 3 by the President of the Senate. In addition, past Presidents of the Republic are, by right, Members of the Constitutional Council.

Legislative power is exercised by Parliament composed of a National Assembly and a Senate. The National Assembly is elected by direct adult suffrage for a 5-year term. All citizens of 18 years may vote. Senators are elected for a 9-year term by an electoral college. One-third of the Senate is re-elected every 3 years.

FRENCH TERRITORIES AND DEPARTMENTS

The overseas departments and territories are integral parts of the French Republic. Each department is administered by a Prefect, with elected General Councils and with elected representatives in the French National Assembly and the Senate of the Republic in France. In the territories, a Governor is appointed by the French Government who is the *ex officio* President of the Council of Government. Territorial Assemblies choose the Vice-President of the Council, if elections are by universal suffrage. Some Members of the Assembly sit in the National Assembly and Senate in France.

Comoro Archipelago

The territory is governed by a Council of Ministers responsible to the Chamber of Deputies, whose 31 Members are elected by universal suffrage.

The Comoro Archipelago is represented in the National Assembly by 2 Deputies, in the Senate by 1 Senator, and in the Economic and Social Council by 1 Councillor.

French Polynesia

The territory is administered by a Governor, a Government Council (over which the Governor presides), consisting of 7 Members elected by the Assembly and a Territorial Assembly of 30 Members elected for a 5-year term on the basis of universal suffrage. French Polynesia is represented in the National Assembly by 1 Deputy, in the Senate by 1 Senator and in the Economic and Social Council by 1 Councillor.

French Territory of Afars and Issas

French Territory of Afars and Issas is administered by a Council of Government of 8 Members. The Council is elected by the Chamber of Deputies which is composed of 32 elected Members. The Territory is represented in the National Assembly and the Senate by 1 Deputy each.

Guadeloupe and Dependencies

In 1946 the status of Guadeloupe was changed to that of an overseas department. The department is under a Prefect and an elected General Council of 36 Members; it is represented in the National Assembly by 3 Deputies, in the Senate by 2 Senators and on the Economic and Social Council by 1 Councillor.

Guiana

In 1946 the status of Guiana was changed to that of an overseas department. It is administered by a Prefect, has an elected Council-General of 16 Members and is represented in the National Assembly and the Senate by 1 Deputy each.

Martinique

In 1946 the status of Martinique was changed to that of an overseas department. The department is under a Prefect. An elected General Council of 36 Members votes the budget, and elective municipal councils administer the communes. Martinique is represented in the National Assembly by 3 Deputies and in the Senate by 2 Senators.

New Caledonia

New Caledonia is administered by a Governor, assisted by a Government Council of 5 which is elected by the Territorial Assembly. The Territorial Assembly is itself an elected body of 35 Members. The Territory is represented in the National Assembly and the Senate by 1 Deputy and 1 Senator.

Réunion

In 1946 the status of Réunion was changed to that of an overseas department. The department is under a Prefect and an elected General Council of 36 Members. Réunion is represented in the National Assembly by 3 Deputies, in the Senate by 2 Senators, and in the Economic and Social Council by 2 Councillors.

St Pierre and Miquelon

The Governor is assisted by a Privy Council consisting of the service chiefs and 2 Members appointed by the Minister of Overseas Territories. A General Council of 14 elected Members was set up by decree of 1946. The Territory is represented in the National Assembly and the Senate by 1 Deputy each.

GABON

Legislative power is exercised by a unicameral National Assembly of 70 Deputies elected by direct suffrage for a 5-year term. In 1968 a one-party government was formally instituted. It normally meets twice a year. The Assembly can be prorogued or dissolved by the President for periods of up to 18 months, after consultation with the Council of Ministers and the President of the Assembly. The President may return a Bill to the Assembly for a second reading when it must be passed by a majority of two-thirds of the Members.

THE GAMBIA

Legislative power is exercised by a unicameral Parliament. The House of Representatives, which is elected for a 5-year term, consists of a Speaker, Deputy Speaker and 32 elected Members; in addition, 4 Chiefs are elected by the Chiefs in Assembly; 3 nominated Members are without votes and the Attorney-General is nominated and has a vote.

GERMAN DEMOCRATIC REPUBLIC (EAST GERMANY)

When the Federal Republic of Germany was established, the People's Council of the Soviet-occupied zone was converted to a provisional People's Chamber (*Volkskammer*). In 1949 the People's Chamber enacted the Constitution of the German Democratic Republic based on the Soviet pattern. All Land Parliaments were abolished in 1952 and replaced by administrative units which do not legislate. All citizens over 18 years have the right to vote. The People's Chamber of 500 Deputies is the supreme organ of state power; it elects the Council of State, the Council of Ministers, the National Defence Council and the judges of the Supreme Court. The maximum term of office is 4 years.

The Council of State consists of a Chairman, 6 Deputy Chairmen, 16 Members and a Secretary. The Council is authorised to issue decrees and decisions with the force of law and to interpret existing laws.

GERMAN FEDERAL REPUBLIC (WEST GERMANY)

The legislature of the Federal Republic comprises the Federal Diet (*Bundestag*) which is elected in universal, adult (at 18 years), direct, free and secret elections for a 4-year term, and the Federal Council (*Bundersrat*), composed of Members of the governments of the *Länder*. The *Bundestag* has 496 Members, and 22 non-voting Members for Berlin. Elections for a new *Bundestag* take place in the last three months of its term, or in the case of its dissolution after not more than 60 days. The new *Bundestag* meets normally not later than 30 days after the election, but must not meet within the electoral period of the previous *Bundestag*. The House itself determines the closure and resumption of its sessions; its President may convene it at an earlier date than that arranged, and is obliged to do so if asked by one-third of its Members, the Federal President or the Federal Chancellor.

Meetings of the *Bundestag* are held in public but the public may be excluded if a motion of one-tenth of the Members or of the Federal Government is passed by a two-thirds majority. Members of the *Bundesrat* and of the Federal Government, as well as persons commissioned by them, shall have access to all meetings of the *Bundestag* and its committees and must be heard at any time. The *Bundestag* itself may demand the presence of any member of the Federal Government.

In between electoral periods the *Bundestag* may set up a Standing Committee to safeguard its rights *vis-à-vis* the Federal Government, and to have the rights of an investigating committee.

The Governments of the *Länder* appoint and recall those of their Members who make up the *Bundesrat*, or they may appoint other Members to represent them. Each *Land* has at least 3 votes; *Länder* with over 2m. inhabitants have 4, those with over 6m. have 5. The *Länder* delegate as many Members as they have votes, and the votes may only be given as a block vote.

The *Bundesrat* elects its own President for 1 year. He convenes the House, and must do so if at least 2 *Länder*, or the Federal Government, demand it. Like the *Bundestag*, the *Bundesrat* normally meets in public, but the public may be excluded. Federal Government has the right to participate in *Bundesrat* debates and committee meetings and must do so if asked. It must also keep the *Bundesrat* informed on the conduct of federal affairs.

Bills are introduced in the *Bundestag* by the Government or by Members of either House. Government Bills go first to the *Bundesrat*, which may give its opinion within three weeks. Federal laws adopted by the *Bundestag* must go also to the *Bundesrat*: within two weeks of receiving the adopted Bill the *Bundesrat* may demand that a joint committee be set up to consider it; the committee's composition and procedure is regulated by Standing Orders agreed by the *Bundestag* with the approval of the *Bundesrat*; Members of the *Bundesrat* serving on this committee are not bound by instructions. If the committee proposes an alteration to the Bill, the *Bundestag* must reconsider. For some laws, *e.g.* laws altering or adding to the Constitution, *Bundesrat* approval is required before the law can be promulgated. For all other laws, the *Bundesrat* has a power of veto which must operate within one week of the law being passed in the *Bundestag*—that is, either one week after the conclusion of proceedings prior to the committee stage, or one week after the receipt of the Bill for reconsideration in the Lower House. If the veto is adopted by the majority of *Bundesrat* votes, it may be rejected by a majority of *Bundestag* votes; if by a two-thirds majority, then the same majority is necessary to reject it, or at least a greater majority than in the former case. Basic law needs the approval of a two-thirds majority in both Houses. *Bundesrat* approval is required for special orders (*Rechtsverordnungen*) of the Federal Government concerning railways, post and telecommunications 'as well as those issued on the basis of federal laws which require the approval of the *Bundesrat* or which are executed by the *Länder* on behalf of the Federation or as their own concern.' (Basic Law of the Federal Republic of Germany, Article 80, para. 2.)

If a government motion to receive a vote of confidence does not obtain the support of the majority of the Members of the *Bundestag*, the President of the Federation may dissolve the House within 21 days. If the House is not dissolved, the President, on the Government's request and with *Bundestag* approval, may declare a state of legislative emergency for a Bill which the House has rejected despite the Government declaring it to be urgent. This also applies if the Bill has been rejected after being put forward combined with a motion for a vote of confidence. If the *Bundestag* rejects the Bill again, or passes it in a version unacceptable to the Government, then the Bill is deemed to be adopted in so far as the *Bundesrat* approves it. The same is held if the Bill has not been passed by the *Bundestag* within four weeks after its re-submission. This does not apply to Bills amending, repealing wholly or partially, or suspending the Basic Law. A Bill rejected for other reasons may, within the term of office of a Chancellor, be passed within six months of the declaration of emergency. After that, a further state of emergency may not be declared during the same Chancellor's term of office.

The Federal Chancellor is elected without discussion by the *Bundestag* on the proposal of the Federal President, and by majority vote. The Ministers are appointed and dismissed by the President on the Chancellor's proposal. The Chancellor determines and assumes responsibility for general policy; each Minister acts on his own responsibility within the terms of this policy. The *Bundestag* may express its lack of confidence in the Chancellor only by electing a successor with the majority of its Members. The office of the Chancellor, or of a Minister, ends in any case with the assembly of a new *Bundestag*.

The Federal President is elected by indirect vote for a five-year term; he may not be a member of the Government or of the legislature; he may be impeached by either House on a two-thirds majority.

The President of the *Bundesrat* is elected by the Members for 1 year, together with his Deputy and the Secretary-General. The President, Deputies and Secretary-General of the *Bundestag* are elected by Members for the duration of their own term.

THE LÄNDER

The state parliaments had considerable autonomy for many years. The Bremen and Hamburg Parliaments had authority since the Middle Ages. The Weimar Constitution of 1919 increased their financial dependence on central government. The National Socialists, in 1933, began to implement a policy of replacing the regional Parliaments with military corps districts which were administrative and not legislative. The Potsdam Conference agreed on decentralisation and restoration of state Parliaments. All contemporary West German state Constitutions are post war, but modelled on those of the Weimar period.

All the Länder follow the same procedural pattern with the exception of Bavaria. Parliaments sit for 4 years and members are elected for the 4-year term. There is 1 Chamber called the *Landtag* (except in Bremen and Hamburg where it is called the *Bürgerschaft*). To qualify as a Member one must be a qualified voter over 25 years. The affairs of the House are managed by a Council of Elders (*Ältestenrat*); this Council arranges calendar and apportions time for Bills introduced, and is headed by the *Landtag* President who is distinct from the Chief Executive.

Bills are introduced anywhere in the House except for finance Bills which are only introduced by the executive. When a Bill has been read for the second time and discussed it is sent to committee, if there has been disagreement, for amendment, and must return to the House to be passed. Parties are strong in *Land* Parliaments, but so are standing committees, these being ordered by the *Ältestenrat* and not by party groups. The Chamber elects the Premier, and he appoints the Cabinet. Election of Members is by proportional representation and universal franchise of all over 21 years.

Baden-Württemberg

Baden-Württemberg was formed in 1951 from a merger of 3 Länder–Baden, Württemberg–Baden and Württemberg–Hohenzollern. The *Landtag*, formed at that time, remains essentially the same with 127 Members.

Bavaria

The Constitution dates from 1946, but was modelled on that of 1919. There are 2 Houses, the Diet and the Senate. The Diet is called the *Landtag*. There are 204 Members of the *Landtag*. Members, who must be qualified voters over 25 years, are elected for a 4-year term. The Senate has 60 Members who must be over 40 years, and are elected for a 6-year term. They may not be Members of the *Landtag* and neither may they represent any Party.

Bills may originate anywhere in the two Houses, except for finance Bills which come only from Ministers. Bills passed in the *Landtag* may not be thrown out in the Senate, which has an advisory function as an expert group. Senate members may suggest amendments to Bills and present objections to them. They give advice which results in the *Landtag* taking action, but they do not themselves amend a Bill and send it back.

Berlin

Berlin (West) was included in the 1950 Constitution as one of the Länder; this followed the setting up of a separate Soviet administration in the Soviet sector in 1948. It has not yet been formally incorporated as a *Land* of the Republic, which means that its representation in the Federal Parliament is not fully effective but its *Land* Parliament is effective as a city government. It is called the House of Representatives; its executive is called the Senate and comprises the first Burgomaster, Deputy Burgomaster and not more than 16 Senators. There are never less than 200 Members. The qualification and election is as for other Länder.

Bremen

The Constitution of 1947 established the present House of Burgesses. The first Constitution allowing a Parliament dates from *c.* 1300. The House, which has 100 Members, appoints an executive which is called the Senate.

Hamburg

The Constitution of 1952 established the present House. The House of Burgesses, which has 120 Members, appoints the executive which is the Senate, under the first Burgomaster.

Hessen

The Constitution came into force in 1946 and established the present House of 96 Members.

Lower Saxony

The present Constitution came into force in 1946 and set up the present House of 149 Members.

North Rhine-Westphalia

The Constitution of 1947 set up the present House of 200 Members.

Rhineland-Palatinate

The Constitution of 1947 set up the present House of 100 Members.

Saarland

A Constitution was passed in 1947 when the Saar was given international status. It became a *Land* of the German Federal Republic in 1957 but the Constitution remained the same, including the provision for a single-chamber Diet with 50 Members.

Schleswig-Holstein

The Constitution of 1947 set up the present House with 73 Members.

GHANA

The Constitution of 1969 was abolished in Jan. 1972 following the army *coup d'état*. All political institutions were abolished and the governing body is the National Redemption Council.

GIBRALTAR

In 1969, following the introduction of a new Constitution, the Legislative and City Councils were merged to produce an enlarged legislature known as the Gibraltar House of Assembly. Membership consists of the Speaker, 15 elected Members and 2 *ex officio* Members, the Attorney-General and the Financial and Development Secretary. Executive authority is exercised by the Governor, who is also Commander-in-Chief. The Governor, while retaining certain reserved powers, is normally required to act in accordance with the advice of the Gibraltar Council, which consists of 4 *ex officio* Members (the Deputy Governor, the Deputy Fortress Commander, the Attorney-General and the Financial and Development Secretary, the Chief Minister and 4 other Members). Elections take place every 4 years and are by universal adult (at 18 years) suffrage.

GILBERT AND ELLICE ISLANDS COLONY

The colony formerly came under the jurisdiction of the High Commissioner for the Western Pacific, but from 1972 has been headed by a Governor with direct access to London. The Gilbert and Ellice Islands Order, 1970, established an Executive Council and a Legislative Council, both of which are presided over by the Resident Commissioner. The former comprises 3 *ex officio* Members (Assistant Resident Commissioner, Attorney-General, Financial Secretary); 2 public service Members; 4 elected Members appointed by the Governor (with the advice of the Leader of Government Business); and the Leader of Government Business, who is elected to the Council by elected Members of the Legislative Council.

The Legislative Council consists of the official Members of the Executive Council plus a further 28 elected Members. It has a 3-year life and its main function is to legislate.

GREECE

The Chamber of Deputies was suspended by the military junta in April 1967. Following the resignation of the military dictatorship in July 1974 it was announced in Aug. that the 1952 Constitution would be reintroduced 'until the country acquires a charter freely approved by the people'.

GUATEMALA

Legislative power is exercised by the President.

GUINEA

The Legislature is unicameral but membership is composed of the one official party, *Parti démocratique de Guinée*. Under the 1963 Constitution, elections are held every 5 years for the 75 Members of the National Assembly. The President and Members can initiate and formulate laws.

GUYANA

The Constitution provides for a republican form of government and the appointment of a President elected by a simple majority vote of the elected Members of the unicameral National Assembly. The exercise of government is through a Prime Minister and a Cabinet responsible collectively to the National Assembly which consists of a Speaker, 53 Members elected on the party list system of proportional representation and on the basis of universal adult suffrage at 21 years, and not more than 6, or such number as Parliament may decide, non-voting Members appointed as Ministers under the Constitution. It has a 5-year term, is presided over by the Speaker, who may or may not be a Member, and is led by the Prime Minister, who is the Member, in the judgement of the President, best able to command the support of the majority in the House.

The more important sections of the Constitution cannot be amended without the support of a majority of voters in a referendum or, in certain circumstances, a two-thirds majority of all Members of the National Assembly.

HAITI

The legislature is unicameral and elections for 58 seats in the Legislative Chamber (*Chambre Législative*) should take place every 6 years as laid down in the Constitution. The Legislative Chamber is known as the National Assembly (*Assemblée Nationale*) for certain specific purposes such as the amendment of the Constitution. Prior to 1961 the Legislature had been bicameral. There is universal adult suffrage at 18 years.

HONDURAS

Until the change of government on 4 Dec. 1972, legislative power had been vested in a single Chamber, the Congress of Deputies, consisting of 64 Members, chosen for 6 years by popular vote, in the ratio of 1 per 30,000 inhabitants. It met for 180 days beginning 26 May and ending 26 Oct. A permanent commission of 5 Members sat while Congress was not in session, for the transaction of routine or emergency business. Executive power is exercised by the President of the Republic. All men and women over 18 are entitled to vote. On 4 Dec. 1972 Congress was suspended and government is by decree.

HONG KONG

The administration is in the hands of a Governor, aided by an Executive Council, composed of the Commander, British Forces; the Colonial Secretary; the Attorney-General; the Secretary for Home Affairs; the Financial Secretary—all of whom are Members *ex officio*; and such other Members, both official and unofficial, as may be appointed by the Queen upon the Governor's nomination. In 1972 there were, in addition to the 5 *ex officio* Members, 1 nominated official and 8 nominated unofficial Members. There is also a Legislative Council, presided over by the Governor, and consisting of not more than 10 official Members, not more than 5 *ex officio* Members, namely, the Colonial Secretary; the Attorney-General; the Secretary for Home Affairs and the Financial Secretary; and not more than 15 nominated unofficial Members. In 1972 there were, in addition to the 5 *ex officio*, 9 official and 14 unofficial Members.

HUNGARY

The legislature is the Parliament (*Országgyülés*), which had 352 Members in 1973. It is elected for a 4-year term by all citizens of 18 years in universal, direct, secret and equal elections. Candidates may stand for election at 18.

More than one candidate may stand in each constituency. No candidate may disagree with the platform of the People's Patriotic Front. All candidates must be approved by a National Election Board, appointed by the People's Patriotic Front. It is the Board's duty to supervise the elections and publish the returns. The right to put up a candidate is vested solely and directly in public nomination meetings which any voter may attend. Any body or individual may nominate a candidate. Candidates with 30 per cent of the votes of those present may stand. To be elected, a candidate must win 50 per cent of the votes at the general election; if he does not, there is a by-election.

Parliament elects a Speaker and 2 Deputy Speakers. It also elects standing committees to report on Bills and other matters as necessary, and may set up *ad hoc* investigatory committees. Parliament elects from among its Members, and may dismiss, the Presidential Council, consisting of a President, 2 Vice-Presidents, a Secretary and 17 Members; and the Council of Ministers. Members have the right of interpellation of Ministers. Members of the Council of Ministers, as leading officers of the executive arm of the State, may not serve upon the Presidential Council.

The Presidential Council convenes Parliament in 2 regular brief sessions each year. Parliament may also be convened at the written demand of two-thirds of all Members. The sittings of Parliament are normally public. A quorum of Parliament is one-half of all Members. Bills are passed by a simple majority of Members present, with the exception that Bills to amend the Constitution require the assenting vote of two-thirds of all Members.

Bills may be proposed by the Presidential Council, the Council of Ministers, Parliamentary Committees or individual Members. Laws once passed are promulgated in the official gazette, *Magyar közlöny*.

The Presidential Council fixes the date of general elections. A new Parliament must be elected not more than 3 months after the dissolution of the old, and convened within one month of the general election. In times of emergency Parliament may dissolve itself before, or prolong itself after, its normal span.

The Presidential Council also supervises the enforcement of the Constitution, and within its competence, may annul or amend administrative measures contrary to the Constitution. It decides in all matters specifically referred to its competence. When Parliament is not in session it exercises the competence of Parliament; its decrees must be approved by Parliament at its next sitting. The Presidential Council continues in office until the election of a new one.

ICELAND

In 1944 the people of Iceland decided, in a referendum, to sever all ties with the Danish Crown. The voters were asked whether they were in favour of the abrogation of the Union Act, and whether they approved of the Bill for a Republican Constitution. The Republic was proclaimed in 1944. The Parliament (*Althingi*) is divided into two Houses, the Upper House and the Lower House. The former is composed of one-third of the Members elected by the whole *Althingi* in common sitting. The remaining two-thirds of the Members form the Lower House. The Members of the *Althingi* receive payment for their services.

The budget Bills must be laid before the two Houses in joint session, but all other Bills can be introduced in either of the Houses. If the Houses do not agree, they assemble in a common sitting and the final decision is given by a majority of two-thirds of the voters, with the exception of budget Bills, where a simple majority is sufficient. The Ministers have free access to both Houses, but can vote only in the House of which they are Members. Bills can be introduced in either House by the Government or by a private Member.

When Bills have been passed by both Houses they are submitted to the President for his signature. All Bills are countersigned by the cabinet minister who is directly responsible.

The electoral law enacted in 1959 provides for an *Althingi* of 60 Members. Of these, 49 are elected in 8 constituencies by proportional representation; the remaining 11 are apportioned to the parties according to their total vote. There is universal adult (at 20 years) suffrage.

INDIA

India is a Union of States and comprises 21 states and 9 Union territories. Each state is administered by a Governor appointed by the President for a 5-year term, while each Union territory is administered by the President through an administrator appointed by him. The head of the Union is the President in whom all executive power is vested, to be exercised on the advice of Ministers responsible to Parliament. He is elected by an electoral college consisting of all the elected Members of Parliament and of the various state legislative assemblies. He holds office for 5 years and is eligible for re-election. He can be removed from office by impeachment for violation of the Constitution. There is also a Vice-President, who is *ex-officio* Chairman of the Upper House of Parliament.

The Parliament for the Union consists of the President, the Council of States (*Rajya Sabha*) and the House of the People (*Lok Sabha*). The Council of States, or the Upper House, consists of not more than 250 Members; in 1974 there were 228 elected Members and 11 Members nominated by the President. The election to this House is indirect; the representatives of each state are elected by the elected Members of the Legislative Assembly of that state. The Council of States is a permanent body not liable to dissolution, but one-third of the Members retire every second year. The House of the People, or the Lower House, consists of not more than 500 Members, directly elected on the basis of adult suffrage (at 21 years) from territorial constituencies in the states, and not more than 25 Members to represent the Union territories, chosen in such manner as Parliament may, by law, provide; in Apr. 1972 there were 518 elected Members and 2 Members nominated by the President.

The House of the People, unless dissolved sooner, continues for a period of 5 years from the date appointed for its first meeting.

For every state there is a legislature which consists of the Governor, and (*a*) 2 Houses, a Legislative Assembly and a Legislative Council, in the states of Andhra Pradesh, Bihar, Jammu and Kashmir, Karnataka, Madhya Pradesh, Maharashtra, Tamil Nadu and Uttar Pradesh, and (*b*) 1 House, a Legislative Assembly, in the other states. Every Legislative Assembly, unless sooner dissolved, continues for 5 years from the date appointed for its first meeting. If the administration cannot continue the Assembly may be suspended or dissolved by the President and the state placed under President's rule. This is normally done at the request of the state government and on the Governor's recommendation. (The dissolution of the Manipur Assembly, in 1974, was exceptional in being against the Governor's advice). Every state Legislative Council is a permanent body and is not subject to dissolution, but one-third of the Members retire every year. Parliament can, however, abolish an existing Legislative Council or create a new one, if the proposal is supported by a resolution of the Legislative Assembly concerned. Legislative Councils have not less than 40 Members, ten-twelfths elected and the rest nominated by the Governor. Legislative Assemblies have between 60 and 500 directly elected Members.

The various subjects of legislation are enumerated in 3 lists in Schedule 7 to the Constitution. List i, the Union List, consists of 97 subjects (including defence, foreign affairs, communications, currency and coinage, banking and customs) with respect to which the Union Parliament has exclusive power to make laws; the state legislature has exclusive power to make laws with respect to the 66 subjects in list ii, the State List–these include police and public order, agriculture and irrigation, education, public health and local government; the powers to make laws with respect to the 47 subjects (including economic and social planning, legal questions and labour and price control) in list iii, the Concurrent List, are held by both Union and state Governments, though the former prevails. But Parliament may legislate with respect to any subject in the State List in circumstances when the subject assumes national importance or during emergencies.

Other provisions deal with the administrative relations between the Union and the states, interstate trade and commerce, distribution of revenues between the States and the Union, official language, etc.

Parliament and the state legislatures are organised according to the following schedule (figures show distribution of seats in Oct. 1972):

	Parliament		State Legislatures	
States:	House of the People (*Lok Sabha*)	Council of States (*Rajya Sabha*)	Legislative Assemblies (*Vidhan Sabhas*)	Legislative Councils (*Vidhan Parishads*)
Andhra Pradesh	41	18	287	90
Assam	14	7	114	—
Bihar	53	22	318	96
Gujarat	24	11	168	—
Haryana	9	5	81	—
Himachal Pradesh	4	3	68	—
Karnataka	27	12	216	63
Kerala	19	9	133	—
Madhya Pradesh	37	16	296	90
Maharashtra	45	19	270	78
Manipur	2	1	60	—
Meghalaya	1	1	60	—
Nagaland	1	1	46	—
Orissa	20	10	140	—
Punjab	13	7	104	40
Rajasthan	23	10	184	—
Tamil Nadu	39	18	234	63
Tripura	2	1	60	—
Uttar Pradesh	85	34	425	108
West Bengal	40	16	280	—
Jammu and Kashmir	6	4	75[2]	36
Union Territories:				
Andaman and Nicobar Islands	1	—	—	—
Arunachal Pradesh	1	—	—	—
Chandigarh	1	—	—	—
Dadra and Nagar Haveli	1	—	—	—
Dehli	7	3	—	—
Goa, Daman and Diu	2	—	30	—
Lacshadweep	1	—	—	—
Mizoram	1	—	30	—
Pondicherry	1	1	30	—
Total	521[1]	229	3,709	664

[1] There are also 2 nominated Members to represent Anglo-Indians.

[2] Excludes 25 seats for Pakistan-occupied areas of the state which are in abeyance.

INDIAN STATES

States have unicameral or bicameral Parliaments, and in all cases Parliament may at any time approve the abolition of or the creation of an Upper House, provided this is supported by a resolution of the Lower

House. States with both a Legislative Council and a Legislative Assembly: Andhra Pradesh, Jammu and Kashmir, Karnataka, Madhya Pradesh, Maharashtra, Tamil Nadu, Uttar Pradesh.

Legislative Councils have not more than one-third of the total Members of the Legislative Assembly, and in no case less than 40 Members. One-third are elected by the Legislative Assembly from persons who are not Legislative Assembly Members, one-third elected by municipal and other local bodies, one-twelfth by teachers and instructors of secondary grade upwards, one-twelfth by graduates of 3 years' standing. The rest are nominated by the Governor. The Houses are permanent and one-third of their Members retire every second year.

Legislative Assemblies have between 60 and 500 Members elected directly. Constituencies are so arranged that the proportion of Members to population is the same throughout the State. Adult universal suffrage applies. Members are elected for a 5-year term.

The state legislatures have exclusive powers over subjects listed in list II of Schedule 7 to the Constitution. All legislation passes through the third reading and committee-stage process. The Upper House may only recommend changes and it must do so within 14 days of receiving a Bill from the Assembly. The Assembly need not heed its recommendations. The Assembly alone may originate money Bills; other measures may be suggested in either House, but seldom are. The Governor may give or withold assent to Bills passed, or he may withhold certain Bills reserving them for the consideration of the Union President.

The state legislatures may be suspended at any time by the Union President and their functions brought under his own control, which happens frequently.

REPUBLIC OF INDONESIA

The highest organ of State is the People's Consultative Assembly (*Madjelis Permusjawaratan Rakjat*). It consists of all Members of the House of Representatives, *Dewan Perwakilan Rakjat,* plus nominated Members, and sits at least once every 5 years to consider constitutional matters and broad lines of policy of the State and the Government.

The legislative body sits at least once a year and Members can submit Bills, if approved by the President. In an emergency the President can enact Ordinances, but these must subsequently be ratified by the *Dewan*, or be revoked.

IRAN

Legislative power is exercised by the Senate and the National Consultative Assembly (*Majles*).

In 1906 the Shah, up to then an absolute ruler, gave his consent to the establishment of a National Assembly, or *Majles,* which drew up a Constitution. This received the Shah's approval on 30 Dec. 1906. The Constitution also provided for the establishment of a Senate, but this body was constituted only in Feb. 1950; 30 of its 60 Members are nominated by the Shah, while the other 30 are elected. As the result of constitutional amendments approved in 1949 and 1957, the number of *Majles* Deputies has been increased from the original 136 to 200 and the term of each *Majles* has been extended from 2 to 4 years; the Shah has the right to dissolve either or both Houses of Parliament and to return to the *Majles* finance Bills for further consideration. All other legislation approved by Parliament the Shah is obliged to sign and promulgate as law.

IRAQ

Legislative power rests with the President and a 5-man Revolutionary Command Council. A National Council of 100 Members selected by the Revolutionary Council was approved by the Revolutionary Command Council in 1973.

IRISH REPUBLIC (ÉIRE)

The National Parliament (*Oireachtas*) consists of the President and two Houses–a House of Representatives (*Dáil Éireann*) and a Senate (*Seanad Éireann*). All laws passed by the *Oireachtas* must conform to the Constitution.

Members of the *Dáil,* who are known as *Teachtaí Dála,* are elected by universal adult suffrage (at 18 years) in a secret ballot, under proportional representation. The *Dáil* has 144 Members and is to be expanded to 148 in the future. An election is held at least every 5 years.

The Senate (*Seanad Éireann*) has 60 Members. Eleven are nominated by the head of the Government, 43 are elected to represent various vocational and cultural interests and 6 are elected by the universities. The powers of the *Seanad* are more restricted than those of the *Dáil*. It may delay a Bill passed by the *Dáil* for a maximum of 90 days, or it may suggest changes in the Bill, but it cannot block such a measure permanently.

The executive power of the State is exercised by the Government, or on its authority. Under the Constitution, the Government must consist of not less than 7, nor more than 15, Members. It acts as a collective authority responsible to the *Dáil*.

The *Taoiseach,* (Prime Minister), is head of the Government and presides over its meetings; the *Tánaiste,* (Deputy Prime Minister), takes the place of the Prime Minister when he is absent or ill. The *Taoiseach,* the *Tánaiste* and the Minister for Finance must be Members of the *Dáil*. Other members of the Government may be Members of either House but not more than two may be drawn from the *Seanad*.

Provision is made in the Constitution for the reference to the people of certain Bills of national importance passed by both Houses of the *Oireachtas*. In such cases a petition may be addressed to the President by a majority of the Members of the *Seanad* and not less than one-third of the Members of the *Dáil*.

ISRAEL

The *Knesset* is a unicameral Parliament with 120 Members. It is elected for a 4-year term by secret ballot and adult (at 18 years) universal direct suffrage. The system of election is by proportional representation. The country is treated as one constituency and the political parties present national lists for the electorate. The voter chooses one of the parties. The strength of the individual parties in the *Knesset* is exactly proportional to their national vote, although a party must win one per cent of the national total in order to gain any seats. There is no system of indicating a preference for an individual candidate.

Bills are generally initiated by the Cabinet, drafted by the Ministry of Justice and presented to the *Knesset* by the Minister concerned. They may also be proposed by a private Member of the *Knesset*. A bill must pass 3 readings before it becomes law.

In general a bill, in order to become law, need be passed by a simple majority of those Members of the *Knesset* present at the time. But any bill affecting the Constitution requires to be accepted by a majority of the whole *Knesset* before becoming law.

ITALY

Parliament consists of a Chamber of Deputies and the Senate. The Chamber is elected for a 5-year term by adult (at 21 years) universal and direct suffrage and it consists of 630 Deputies. The Senate is elected by adult (at 25 years) universal suffrage for a 5-year term on a regional basis, each region having at least 6 Senators, with a total membership of 315 elected Senators; the Valle d'Aosta is represented by 1 Senator only. The President of the Republic can nominate 5 Senators for life from eminent men in the social, scientific, artistic and literary spheres. Senators must be at least 40 years of age. On the expiry of his term of office, the President of the Republic becomes a Senator by right and for life, unless he declines.

The Constitution provided for the division of Italy into 20 autonomous regions (*regioni*). Five of these regions (Sicily, Sardinia, Aosta, Trentino-Alto Adige, and Friuli-Venezia Giulia) have a special statute (*regioni autonome con statuto speciale*).

These special regions have their own Parliaments (*consiglio regionale*) and Governments (*giunta regionale e presidente*) with certain legislative and administrative functions adapted to the circumstances of each region.

Bills may be initiated by the Government, Members of both Houses and certain organizations such as the National Council of Economy and Labour and Regional Government. The people can exercise initiative in legislation through a Bill supported by at least 50,000 voters. Every Bill submitted to one of the Houses is examined by a Committee and then by the Chamber itself which approves it, article by article, and subsequently with a final vote. Laws are promulgated by the President of the Republic within a month of their having been voted. If the two Chambers, each with an absolute majority among its own members, declare a Bill to be urgent, it is promulgated within the time laid down in the Bill itself. Laws are published immediately after they have been promulgated and come into force on the fifteenth day after their publication, unless the laws themselves provide otherwise.

IVORY COAST

Legislative power is exercised in a National Assembly of 100 Members on a single-party system. The election of members by adult (at 21 years) suffrage for a 5-year term, takes place at the time of the Presidential election. Legislation may be introduced by the President or by a Member of the National Assembly.

JAMAICA

The Parliament of Jamaica consists of HM the Queen, represented by the Governor-General, the House of Representatives and the Senate.

The House of Representatives consists of 53 Members elected on the basis of universal adult suffrage and any Commonwealth citizen of 18 years or over, who has been living in Jamaica for the 12 months preceding an election, may become a Member of the House of Representatives or the Senate. There is a Constitutional provision that the membership may be increased to 60.

The House of Representatives is the more powerful of the two Houses.

The government of the day can only exist if it has the support of the majority of the Members in the House of Representatives; it must be prepared to defend its policy and all its actions in the House. Although any Bill, other than money Bills, may be introduced into the Senate, major legislation is always introduced in the House of Representatives. Further, no Bill may become law unless it is passed by a majority of the Members present in the House. The House of Representatives has control over the Government's finances; no supply of funds may be granted nor taxation levied without the approval of the House.

The Senate is made up of 21 nominated Senators. Thirteen Senators are appointed by the Governor-General on the advice of the Prime Minister; 8 are appointed by the Governor-General on the advice of the Leader of the Opposition. The Senate allows for full consideration and revision of every Bill passed by the House before it becomes law.

JAPAN

The Diet is the highest organ of state power and the only law-making body. It consists of 2 Houses, the House of Representatives (*Shugi-in*) with 491 Members and the House of Councillors (*Sangi-in*), formerly the House of Peers with 251 Members: The Members of the House of Representatives are elected for a 4-year term, but their tenure of office is terminated with a dissolution of the House. The Members of the House of Councillors are elected for a 6-year term, with one-half elected every 3 years. 100 of the Members of the House of Councillors are elected by the national constituency, while the remainder are elected by prefectural constituencies. Members of the House of Representatives are elected by what is called 'the medium constituency', which is between the local and prefectural electorate and is based on population as at 1945 and as population distribution has changed the subsequent inbalance is actively under discussion.

Bills can be presented either by the Cabinet or by Diet members. However, the normal Japanese practice is an unusual one, most Bills have so far been introduced by the Cabinet with scarcely any bills presented by Diet members. Exceptional bills of the latter type are usually specially referred to as Diet members' Bills.

The President of the House of Councillors and the Speaker of the House of Representatives usually institute a committee consisting of a number of Diet members to deliberate on the Bills which have been presented. Later, the Bills are submitted for discussion by plenary sessions of all members of each House.

The voting age is 20 years and above for all citizens. Every Diet Member is assigned to at least one committee. These committees examine closely and deliberate in detail all the Bills, petitions, representations and other matters which come under their respective spheres of responsibility.

A Bill is enacted into law with the approval by both Houses of the Diet, but the House of Representatives has been granted supremacy in certain instances. For example, in the case of the budget and the approval of treaties, the vote of the House of Representatives is the vote of the Diet when the decision of the two Houses differs and they fail to reach agreement, or when the House of Councillors fails to act within 30 days after notification of the action taken by the House of Representatives.

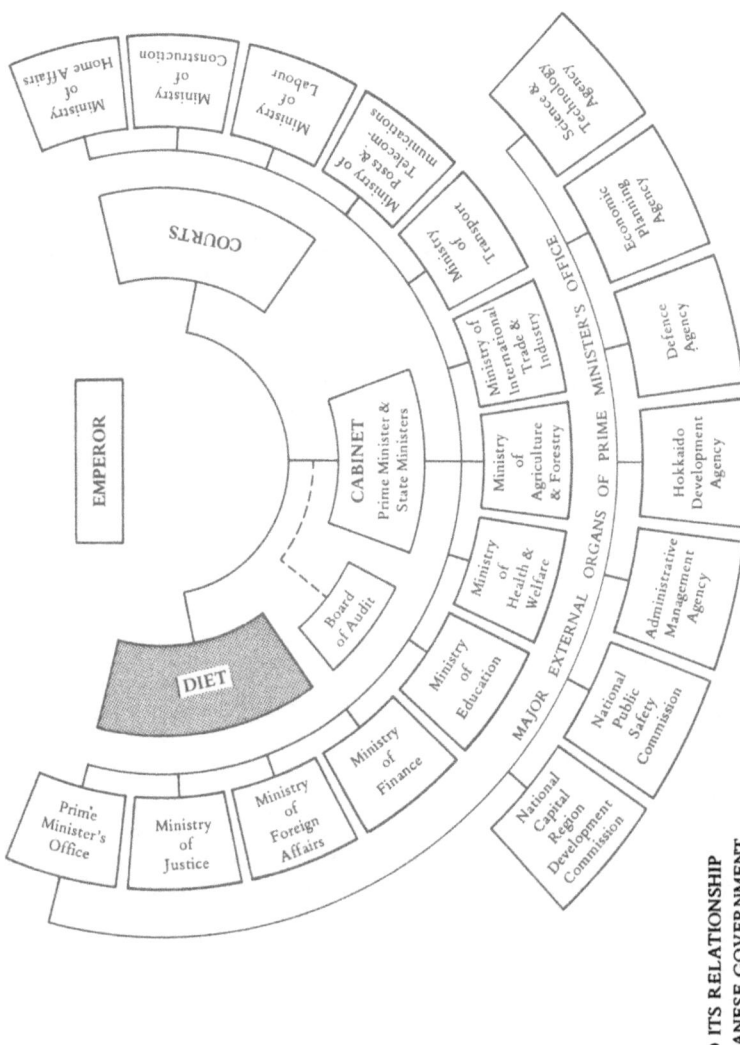

THE DIET AND ITS RELATIONSHIP
WITH THE JAPANESE GOVERNMENT

JORDAN

Legislative power is exercised by the National Assembly (*Majlis el-Umma*) and the King. The Senate or Chamber of the Appointed (*Majlis el-A'yaan*) and the House of Deputies (*Majlis en Nuwwaab*) constitutes the National Assembly. The number of Senators is half the number of the House of Representatives. Senators must be over 40 years and unrelated to the King, and are appointed for a 4-year term. Members of the House of Deputies, who must be over 30 years, are elected for a 4-year term by secret ballot by adult (at 20 years) suffrage. Decisions in both Houses are taken by a majority vote, with a quorum of two-thirds of Members present.

If Bills, presented by the Prime Minister, are accepted by the House of Deputies, they go to the Senate and then to the King for confirmation. If one House accepts a Bill but the other House rejects it, a joint session is called and a two-third majority decision is taken. Should the King use his prerogative and withhold approval of a Bill, he returns it, with reasons for withholding approval, within 6 months, and then both Houses meet together to make a decision.

KENYA

Parliament is unicameral and is called the National Assembly. It has 158 elected Members, including the President, 12 Members nominated by the President, and two *ex officio* Members–the Speaker, elected by the National Assembly, and the Attorney-General, a civil servant appointed by the President. An elected or nominated Member must be a Kenya citizen of not less than 21 years and must be registered as a voter. Parliament is for a 5-year term but may be dissolved sooner by the President. Candidates for National Assembly elections, unless nominated unopposed, are selected at party preliminary elections at which any registered voter who declares himself to be a member or supporter of the party may vote. While only one political party exists, no polling takes place at parliamentary or presidential elections but only at preliminary elections. There is universal adult (at 18 years) suffrage. In July 1974 Swahili became the official language for use in the National Assembly.

KHMER REPUBLIC (CAMBODIA)

A Republican Constitution providing for a bicameral Parliament (*Sepiacheat*), consisting of a National Assembly (*Rathsepia*) with 126 Deputies elected for a 4-year term, and a Senate (*Pritsepia*), with 40 Members elected for a 6-year term was adopted by referendum in 1972. There is universal adult (at 18 years) suffrage. Parliament was suspended in 1973.

DEMOCRATIC PEOPLE'S REPUBLIC OF KOREA (NORTH KOREA)

The Constitution of 1972 provides for a Supreme People's Assembly of 541 Deputies elected by universal suffrage. In practice the country is ruled by the Korean Workers' (*i.e.* Communist) Party, which elects the Central Committee which, in turn, elects the Politburo. Legislative enactments are approved when adopted by more than 50 per cent of Deputies present. The Standing Committee is the permanent body of the Supreme People's Assembly and it examines and decides on Bills, amends laws when the Supreme People's Assembly is not in session.

REPUBLIC OF KOREA (SOUTH KOREA)

The legislative authority is the unicameral National Assembly consisting of a minimum of 150 and a maximum of 250 Members. In 1974 there were 146 elected Members for a period of 6 years and 73 Members elected by the Unification Conference serving for 3 years. Voting is by adult (at 20 years) suffrage.

KUWAIT

The Ruler of Kuwait and Head of State is the Amir. The Amir appoints the Prime Minister and the Council of Ministers. The legislative authority is the National Assembly. There are 50 Members who are elected for a 4-year term by literate males over 21 years. Candidates must be over 30 years. The Amir may ask for a Bill, sent to him for ratification, to be reconsidered, but the Bill becomes law if passed by a two-third majority at the next sitting of the National Assembly, or by a simple majority at a subsequent sitting.

LAOS

The legislature consists of an advisory King's Council and a National Assembly of 59 Members. Elections are held every 5 years by universal suffrage.

LEBANON

Legislative power is exercised by a unicameral Parliament, the Chamber of Deputies, consisting of 99 Members. Seats are allocated to 54 Christians and 45 Muslims as laid down in the electoral law. Members are elected by universal suffrage and must be over 25 years. Voting is at 21 years. The term of the Chamber is generally 4 years. A quorum is two-thirds and a majority vote is required on Constitutional matters. Initiative for legislation rests with the President of the Republic and with the Chamber of Deputies.

LESOTHO

Parliament consists of the National Assembly of 60 Members elected by adult suffrage, and a Senate of 22 principal Chiefs and 11 Members nominated by the King.

The elections of 1970 were declared invalid and the Constitution suspended.

LIBERIA

The Constitution of the Republic is modelled on that of the USA. Legislative power lies with a bicameral Parliament. The Senate has 18 Members elected for a 6-year term, and the House of Representatives has 65 Members elected for a 4-year term.

LIBYAN ARAB REPUBLIC

Libya is a democratic and free Arab Republic and authority rests with the Revolutionary Command Council. The National Assembly has been abolished.

LIECHTENSTEIN

Since 1921 the Constitution has provided for a Diet (*Landtag*) of 15 Members elected for a 4-year term by direct vote on the basis of universal suffrage and proportional representation. The reigning Prince exercises the legislative right jointly with the *Landtag*. All male citizens of 20 years and over may vote.

The right of legislative initiative lies with the Prince, the Diet and citizens with the right to vote. If no less than 600 citizens entitled to vote submit a petition in writing, or if at least 3 communes do so in the form of resolutions of the communal assembly, requesting the enactment, modification or revocation of a law, such petition must be debated at the next sitting of the Diet.

A law becomes valid when it receives the assent of the Diet, is sanctioned by the Prince, countersigned by the responsible Head of Government or his deputy and published in the *Landesgesetzblatt*.

LUXEMBOURG

The Grand Duchy of Luxembourg is a constitutional monarchy, the hereditary sovereignty being the Massau family. The Parliament consists of 59 Members elected for a 5-year term. An elector must be a Luxembourg national and be over 18 years; to be elegible for election the citizen must be 21 years. There is also a Council of State of 21 Members nominated by the Sovereign, which is the supreme administration authority and also fulfills certain legislative functions. The Head of State takes part in the legislative power, exercises the executive power and has a certain part in the judicial power. The Constitution leaves to the Sovereign the right to organise the Government. Bills are passed after 2 readings with an interval of 3 months between them, if they are approved by an absolute majority.

MADAGASCAR (THE MALAGASY REPUBLIC)

The Presidential form of government adopted under the 1959 Constitution was suspended in 1972 for a 5-year period. The Head of Government rules by Ordinance.

MALAWI

Parliament is unicameral consisting of a National Assembly, and has a 5-year term. It has 63 elected Members and, in addition, the President may appoint up to 15 nominated Members. All Members must belong to the Malawi Congress Party. Adult suffrage is at 21 years.

MALAYSIA

The Federal Parliament of Malaysia is bicameral and comprises the *Yang Dipertuan Agung,* the Sovereign, the House of Representatives (*Dewan Ra'ayat*) and the Senate (*Dewan Negara*). Malaysia is a federation of 13 states.

The *Dewan Ra'ayat* consists of 144 Members–104 from Peninsula Malaysia, 24 from Sarawak and 16 from Sabah. The House of Representatives has a 5-year term.

The *Dewan Negara* has a membership of 58, made up of 26 elected and 32 appointed Members. Each state legislature, acting as an electoral college, elects 2 Senators. They may be Members of the State Legislative Assembly or otherwise. The *Yang Dipertuan Agung* appoints the other 32 Members. The Legislative Assembly of Sabah consists of a Speaker, 32 elected Members and not more than 6 nominated Members. The *Council Negri,* or Legislature of Sarawak, consists of 48 elected Members who sit for a 5-year term.

REPUBLIC OF THE MALDIVES

The President is elected for a 4-year term by universal adult suffrage, and appoints his own Cabinet. The Cabinet is responsible to the House of Representatives (*Majlis*) which consists of 54 Members elected for a 5-year term.

MALI

A National Liberation Committee assumed all political and administrative functions in 1968. A Constitution referendum was held in June 1974. Under this Constitution, the President and the Head of Government would be elected by universal suffrage for a period not exceeding two 5-year terms. A National Assembly would be elected for a 4-year term and a sole political party constituted. The Constitution also laid down that for a period of 5 years the Military Committee of National Liberation would 'define and conduct the policy of the State'.

MALTA

By the Malta Independence Order, 1964, the Parliament of Malta, consisting of HM the Queen and a House of Representatives, was established. The Governor-General of Malta is appointed by Her Majesty and holds office during HM pleasure and is HM representative in Malta.

The House of Representatives consists of 55 Members known as Members of Parliament who serve for a maximum of 5 years between elections. A person is qualified to be elected as a Member of the House of Representatives if he is a Maltese citizen, resident in Malta, and over 21 years. The Members of the House are elected upon the principle of proportional representation by means of the single transferable vote.

MAURITANIA

The National Assembly is elected by universal suffrage for a 5-year term. Citizens must be 25 years to become Members of the Assembly. Mauritania is a one-party State and the President decides and conducts the policy of the State.

MAURITIUS

The Legislative Assembly consists of a Speaker and 62 elected Members, 3 each for the 20 constituencies of Mauritius and 2 for Rodrigues, and 8 additional seats in order to ensure a fair and adequate representation of each community within the Assembly. General elections are held every 5 years on the basis of universal adult suffrage.

MEXICO

Mexico is a Federal Republic with a Constitution similar to that of the USA. It is divided into 29 states each of which has the right to manage its own local affairs. Citizenship, including the right of suffrage, is vested in all nationals of 18 years and who have 'an honourable means of livelihood'; women were given equal citizenship and suffrage with men in 1952–3. Thumbprints are taken of registered voters.

Congress consists of a Chamber of Deputies elected for 3 years by universal suffrage, and a Senate of 60 Members, 2 for each state and the federal district, elected for a 6-year term. Since 1964 additional 'party deputies' have also been elected to the Chamber according to a system of partial proportional representation. There are (1973) 216 seats, of which the 3 small opposition parties hold 35. Senators and Deputies are ineligible for re-election until another term has elapsed. Congress sits from 1 Sept. to 31 Dec. During the recess there is a permanent committee consisting of 14 Senators and 15 representatives appointed by the respective Houses.

MONACO

Legislative power is exercised by the Prince and the National Council. The Council has 18 Members, elected for a 5-year term by universal adult (at 21 years) suffrage. The minimum age for Members is 25 years. The initiative rests with the Prince, but the National Council may submit draft proposals to him and ask him to initiate them. The National Council controls the budget, which is submitted to it by the Council, and has sole right to levy direct taxation.

MONGOLIAN PEOPLE'S REPUBLIC

Under the 1960 Constitution power is vested in the *People's Great Khural* of Deputies, elected for a 3-year term by universal suffrage of voters over 18 years on a basis of 1 Deputy per 2,500 inhabitants. It elects from its number 9 Members of the Presidium, which carries on current state affairs. *De facto* power is in the hands of the only political party, the Mongolian People's Revolutionary (*i.e.,* Communist) Party.

MONTSERRAT

The Legislative Council consists of the Governor, 7 elected Members, and one nominated Member and the Attorney-General and Financial Secretary.

MOROCCO

Parliament is bicameral comprising a House of Representatives and a House of Counsellors. Members of the House of Representatives are elected for a 4-year term by direct universal suffrage. Two-thirds of the Members of the House of Counsellors are elected in each prefecture and province by an electoral college composed of Members of prefectoral and provincial assemblies and communal councils; one-third are elected by the Chambers of Agriculture, Commerce and Industry, Handicrafts, and by trade unions. Candidates must be Members of the Chamber or Union concerned. Members are elected for a 6-year term and half their number are re-elected every 3 years.

The Prime Minister and the Members of Parliament are empowered to introduce Bills. If the Representatives reject a Bill after its first reading, the Government may refer it to the House of Counsellors. Government and Members have the right of amendment; after debate has opened the Government may oppose the examination of any amendment which has not been previously submitted to the appropriate committee. The Government may also require the House to give a ruling after a single vote on all, or part of, the text, retaining only those amendments submitted or approved by the Government. All Bills are examined by both Houses. If a Bill has not been passed after two readings in each House, or if the Government invokes emergency procedure after a single reading by one of them, the Bill shall be re-submitted to the House of Representatives and a two-thirds majority approves or rejects it. A text which is approved is submitted to the King's final decision. Fundamental laws are tabled, but not debated or voted on for at least ten days. The procedure of re-submission does not apply to them.

The King may ask for a further reading of a measure submitted for his assent, but his request must be countersigned by the Prime Minister. By royal decree he may submit any proposed legislation to referendum so long as it has been discussed in both Houses. The results of a referendum are binding on the whole of the Parliament. If a Bill rejected by Parliament is approved by referendum, then the House of Representatives is automatically dissolved. However, no motion to alter the Constitution may be promulgated until it has been approved by referendum.

NAURU

There are 18 Members of Parliament, formerly called Legislative Assembly. Voting is compulsory for those over 20 years.

NEPAL

The Parliament (*Rashtriya Panchayat*) is unicameral and comprises 125 Members. The village and town *Panchayat,* recognised as the basic units of democracy, elect the district *Panchayat,* these elect the zonal *Panchayat,* and these finally the 90 Members of the national *Panchayat.* In addition, 19 representatives of professional organisations and university graduates, and royal nominees not exceeding 15 per cent of the elected Members, will be included in the national *Panchayat.* The executive power is vested in the King, who appoints a Council of Ministers from the national *Panchayat.* A State Council will advise the King and proclaim the successor or, if the heir is a minor, a Regency Council. Article 81 empowers the King to declare a state of emergency, and to suspend the Constitution. Members can move, reject or pass with or without amendment, any Bill except those concerned with the royal family and the armed forces. Members may initiate legislation, but for money Bills and defence matter prior approval by the King is necessary.

THE NETHERLANDS

The States-General comprises a First Chamber of 75 Members and Second Chamber of 150 Deputies, the Second Chamber being the more important of the two.

The legislative power is exercised by the Crown and the States-General *(Staten Generaal)*. The Members of the Second Chamber are elected for a 4-year term, and retire in a body, whereas the First Chamber is elected for a 6-year term, one-half retiring every 3 years in rotation. There is universal adult (at 18 years) suffrage. The Sovereign has the power to dissolve both Chambers of Parliament, or one of them, subject to the conditions that new elections take place within 40 days, and the new House or Houses be convoked within 3 months. The Sovereign transmits Bills submitted by the responsible Minister(s) to the Second Chamber after they have been discussed in the Council of Ministers and the Council of State has made its recommendations. When Bills have been passed by the Second Chamber, they go to the First Chamber. The Government is entitled to recall Bills which have been laid before Parliament. While a Bill is before the Second Chamber both the Government and the Second Chamber may amend it. Some very exceptional subjects have to be dealt with in joint sittings of the First and Second Chambers, in which case the combined sitting has the right of amendment.

When a law applicable equally to Surinam, or the Netherlands Antilles, or both, and to the Netherlands in Europe, is to be passed by the legislature, a Kingdom Bill is submitted to the States-General, which then acts as the Parliament of the Kingdom. After the Bill has been signed by the Queen and countersigned by the Minister or Ministers responsible, it becomes a Kingdom Act. The Queen sends the Bill simultaneously to the States-General and to the Representative Body of Surinam, or the Netherlands Antilles, or both. The latter have the right to examine the Bill and, if necessary, report their findings within a specified period of time, before it is publicly debated in the States-General.

The Ministers Plenipotentiary of the countries to which the law will apply are given the opportunity to attend the debates on the Bill in the States-

General, and to participate in them as they consider necessary. The Representative Bodies of the countries concerned have the right to send special delegates to the sittings of the States-General at which the Bill is to be debated, so that they too may furnish the Chambers with such information on the subject as they think fit.

The Ministers Plenipotentiary and the special representatives are entitled to amend the Bill during the debates in the Second Chamber of the States-General. Before the Bill is voted in the States-General, the Ministers Plenipotentiary of the countries to which the law will apply are afforded the opportunity of expressing their opinion on the proposals contained in the Bill. Should a Minister Plenipotentiary oppose the Bill, he may request the Chamber to postpone voting on it to a subsequent sitting. If the Chamber passes the Bill despite the Minister Plenipotentiary's opposition, but with a majority of less than three-fifths of the votes cast, the debate in the Chamber will be suspended and further consultations will be held by the Council of Ministers of the Kingdom. When a special representative is present during the debates in the Second Chamber, the Minister Plenipotentiary's right to oppose a Bill passes to him.

The Constitution can be revised only by a Bill declaring that there is reason for introducing such revision, and containing the proposed alterations. The passing of this Bill is followed by a dissolution of both Chambers, and a second confirmation by the new States-General by two-thirds of the votes.

The Netherlands Antilles

The executive power in internal affairs rests with the Governor and the Council of Ministers, who together form the Government. The Ministers are responsible to the unicameral legislature *(Staten)*. This consists of 22 Members: 12 from Curaçao; 8 from Aruba; 1 from Bonaire; 1 from the Windward Islands; and is elected by universal adult suffrage.

In 1951 the Netherlands Antilles Islands Regulation provided for self-government of each of the 4 insular communities of Aruba, Bonaire, Curaçao and the Windward Islands. The autonomous powers of the insular communities are divided between the Island Council, which is elected by universal adult suffrage, the Executive Council and the Lieutenant-Governor *(Gezaghebber)*, who is responsible for maintaining public peace and order.

Surinam

There is a Council of 13 Ministers who are responsible to the Legislative Council *(Staten van Suriname)*. The Legislative Council of 39 Members is elected for a 4-year term by universal adult suffrage.

NEW ZEALAND

Parliament is unicameral and consists of a House of Representatives, the former Legislative Council having been abolished in 1951.

The voting age is 20 years for all persons of over one year's residence and of British and Irish citizenship. The House of Representatives consists of 87 Members, including 4 Maoris, elected by the people for a 3-year term. The 4 Maori electoral districts cover the whole country and adult Maoris of half-blood or more are the electors. A half-caste Maori is entitled to register either for a European or a Maori electoral district. Women's suffrage was instituted in 1893; women became eligible as Members of the House of Representatives in 1919. The House in 1973 included 4 women Members.

NICARAGUA

In 1971 the Congress was dissolved. A 100-member Constituent Assembly started its discussion on a new Constitution in 1972.

NIGER

The National Assembly was unicameral and consisted of a single party of 50 Members elected for a 5-year term by universal adult suffrage. On 14 April 1974 the Constitution was suspended and the National Assembly dissolved.

NIGERIA

Since March 1967 legislative and executive power has been vested in the Federal Military Government consisting of a Supreme Military Council and a Federal Executive Council. Except for the East Central State, which is ruled by an Administrator, each state is ruled by a Military Governor who presides over the State Executive Council, which includes some civilians.

NORWAY

Norway is a constitutional and hereditary monarchy. The royal succession is in direct male line in the order of primogeniture. In default of male heirs, the King may propose a successor to the *Storting*, but this assembly has the right to nominate another if it does not agree with the proposal.

The *Storting* assembles every year. The meetings take place *suo jure*, and not by any writ from the King or the executive. They begin on the first week-day in October each year, and their duration is not limited. Every Norwegian subject of 20 years (provided that he resides, and has resided for 5 years, in the country) is entitled to vote, unless he is disqualified for a special cause. Women are, since 1913, entitled to vote under the same conditions as men. The mode of election is direct and the method of election is proportional. The country is divided into 19 districts, each electing from 4 to 15 representatives. The total number of representatives is 155.

The *Storting* when assembled, divides itself by election into the *Lagting* and the *Odelsting*. The former is composed of one-fourth of the Members of the *Storting*, and the other of the remaining three-fourths. Each *Ting* (the *Storting*, the *Odelsting* and the *Lagting*) nominates its own President. Most questions are decided by the *Storting*, but questions relating to legislation must be considered and decided by the *Odelsting* and the *Lagting* separately. Only when the *Odelsting* and the *Lagting* disagree, the Bill has to be considered by the *Storting* in plenary sitting, and a new law can then be decided only by a majority of two-thirds of the voters. The same majority is required for alterations of the Constitution, which can be decided only by the *Storting* in plenary sitting.

OMAN

The Sultan has an advisory Council of Ministers. The legislative process is by decree.

PAKISTAN

A Constitution was adopted by the National Assembly on 10 Apr. 1973. The Constitution envisaged a bicameral legislature. The National Assembly would have 210 Members, 10 seats being reserved for women. Election is by universal adult (at 18 years) suffrage for a maximum term of 5 years. The Senate has 60 Members and is mainly advisory. It may send back once, for reconsideration, legislation proposed by the National Assembly. In the case of deadlock, the 2 Houses would sit in joint session and the Bill would become law on a simple majority vote. Constitutional changes would need two-thirds majority in the National Assembly and a simple majority in the Senate.

PANAMA

In 1972 a 505-member Assembly was directly elected to approve a new Constitution. Under this Constitution there is an indirectly elected President, Vice-President and Legislative Council, but full executive powers were given to General Torrijos for a 6-year period as a 'transitory provision' of the Constitution. There is universal adult suffrage and the vote is equal and secret. Adult suffrage is at 18 years.

PAPUA NEW GUINEA

The Papua New Guinea Act, 1949–1972, provides for the administration of the UN Australian Trust Territory of New Guinea in an administrative union with the Territory of Papua, in accordance with Article 5 of the New Guinea Trusteeship Agreement, under the title of Papua New Guinea. The Act, which is administered by the Minister of State for External Territories, provides for the appointment of an Administrator to administer the government of Papua New Guinea on behalf of the Commonwealth of Australia.

In 1968 the Papua New Guinea Act was amended to provide for the Administrator's Council to become the Administrator's Executive Council, deciding major matters of policy. In June 1968 it had its first meetings. It consists of the Administrator, the 7 ministerial Members, 3 official Members, and a twelfth Councillor who is an elected MHA nominated by the Administrator. From Aug. 1970, ministerial office-holders have been responsible for day-to-day running of their departments. In addition (subject to the Administrator's Executive Council), they exercise full authority in a substantial number of specific matters. The Commonwealth Government has retained authority in defence, foreign affairs, trade, the judiciary, major development projects and non-specific matters. The House of Assembly was established in 1964 and has 100 Members, elected by residents over 18 years, and 4 official Members. Papua New Guinea obtained self-government in Dec. 1973 and full independence is envisaged in 1974 or 1975.

PARAGUAY

A new Constitution replacing that of 1940 was drawn up by a Constituent Convention in which all legally recognised political parties were represented, and was signed into law on 25 Aug. 1967. It provides for a two-chamber Parliament consisting of a 30-seat Senate and a 60-seat Chamber of Deputies. Two-thirds of the seats in each Chamber are allocated to the majority party, and the remaining one-third shared among the minority parties in proportion to the votes cast. Voting is compulsory for all citizens over 18 years.

PERU

The Constitution provides for a legislature consisting of a Senate (*Camara de Senadores*) of 45 Members over 35 years and a Chamber of Deputies (*Camara de Diputades*) of 140 Members over 25 years, and an executive formed of the President of the Republic and a Council of Ministers appointed by him. Elections are to be held every 6 years with the President and Congress elected, at the same time, by separate ballots. All literate Peruvians, native-born or naturalised and over 21 years, are eligible to vote.

REPUBLIC OF THE PHILIPPINES

A new Constitution was approved by referendum in Jan. 1973. Martial law was re-introduced and Congress suspended, being replaced by Citizens' Assemblies or *barangays*.

POLAND

The legislature is the *Sejm* and consists of 460 Deputies elected by all citizens of 18 years or over, by equal, direct and secret suffrage for a 4-year term. 616 candidates are permitted to stand for the 460 seats. Constituencies are of equal size. Candidates for the *Sejm* must be 21 years or over.

The *Sejm* elects a Marshal and Deputy Marshals, and sets up Commissions as necessary. The Commissions' tasks include reporting to the *Sejm* on Bills, and receiving information and reports from executive departments. The Commissions present proposals to the *Sejm* in session, and do not themselves enact laws. The debates of the *Sejm* are open to the public, unless it is voted otherwise.

At its first sitting the *Sejm* elects from among its Members the Council of State, composed of a Chairman, 4 Deputy Chairmen, a Secretary and 11 Members. The Council of State orders the holding of elections to the *Sejm*, lays down binding interpretations of the laws, and ratifies and denounces international treaties. It convenes the *Sejm* in 2 regular sessions per year, lasting about two weeks each, and is bound to convene an extraordinary session on a written motion by one-third of the total number of Deputies. In the intervals between the *Sejm's* sessions, the Council of State issues decrees having the force of law, which must be submitted for the *Sejm's* approval at its next session. The first session of a newly-elected *Sejm* must be held not later than one month after the elections. The Council of State orders the holding of elections to the *Sejm* not later than one month before the expiry of the latter's term of office, the date of the election being fixed for a non-working day within two months after the expiry of the term of office. After the expiry of the *Sejm's* term, the Council of State acts until the election of a new Council of State by the newly-elected *Sejm*.

Bills may be introduced by the Government, the Council of State or by Deputies. Laws passed by the *Sejm* are published in the journal of laws (*Dziennik ustaw*). The Constitution may be amended only by a majority of not less than two-thirds of the votes, not less than one-half of the total number of Deputies being present.

Deputies may make interpellations of Ministers, which have to be answered within 7 days.

PORTUGAL

In April 1974 the 'Movement of the Armed Forces' overthrew the government and on 26 April the President announced the dissolution of National Assembly.

In 1933 the present Constitution, which declares that the Portuguese State is a unitary and corporative republic, was adopted by plebiscite. The President is elected for a 7-year term by an electoral college constituted of Members of the National Assembly and the Corporative Chamber, with representatives of municipalities and overseas Legislative Councils. The National Assembly, which is unicameral, has 130 Deputies elected for a 4-year term by direct suffrage. Angola and Mozambique are represented by 7 Deputies each, Portuguese India by 3, Cape Verde by 2, Guinea, S. Tomé and Principe, Macao, Timor by 1 each. A State Council composed of the Prime Minister, the Presidents of the National Assembly, the Corporative Chamber and the Supreme Court, the Public Prosecutor and 10 other Members, assists the President of the Republic. A Corporative Chamber functions alongside the National Assembly.

STATES AND OVERSEAS TERRITORIES

Following the April 1974 *coup d'état* the President of the Republic announced on 27 July that Portugal was prepared to offer independence to her African overseas territories of Angola, Mozambique and Portuguese Guinea.

Greater autonomy 'without affecting the unity of the nation' was granted to the overseas territories in 1973. The principal provisions were that Angola and Mozambique would be designated as states, instead of overseas provinces; they would thus have the same status as the former 'State of India' (Goa, Damão and Diu), which is still officially regarded as Portuguese and has representation in the National Assembly, although annexed in 1961. Each state would continue to be headed by a Governor-General, who would, as hitherto, be nominated by the Lisbon Government but who would in future have the rank of Minister of State in any part of the nation, and could be called to Cabinet meetings. The Governor-General would hold office for a 4-year term, with possible extensions for further 2-year periods. Angola and Mozambique would each have its own elected Legislative Assembly, as well as a consultative council which would assist the Governor-General in the day-to-day business of government. The Legislative Assemblies would meet twice annually for periods not exceeding 4 months a year. While the Governor-General would retain the right of veto, the

Legislative Assemblies could, by a two-thirds majority, block projects put forward, thus invoking arbitration by the central Government. The overseas states, which in addition to electing their own governing bodies would send more representatives than hitherto to the National Assembly in Lisbon, would legislate on all their home affairs, collect their own taxes, and be responsible for their own budgets. The central Government would, however, retain the right of appointing diplomatic representatives and making treaties with foreign states, and would also have the authority to supervise the administration and economy of the overseas states, as well as remaining responsible for their defence.

Statehood was not granted by the legislation to Portugal's other overseas possessions—*i.e.* Guinea (Bissau), the Cape Verde Islands, the islands of S. Tomé and Principe, Macao, and Portuguese Timor.

Under the Organic Law, the Legislative Assemblies of Angola and Mozambique would have 53 and 50 Members respectively; that of the Cape Verde Islands 21; those of Guinea and the S. Tomé and Principe Islands, 17 and 16 Members respectively; that of Timor 20 Members; and that of Macao 13 Members, one of whom would be specially entrusted with the interests of the Chinese community and would be appointed by the Governor.

QATAR

A Consultative Assembly has 23 Members. An Advisory Council was set up in 1972 consisting of 16 Members. All Members must be at least 24 years and their function is to debate draft laws proposed by the Council of Ministers before their submission to the Head of State for ratification and promulgation.

RHODESIA

Prior to Oct. 1923 Southern Rhodesia was under the administration of the British South Africa Company. In Oct. 1922 Southern Rhodesia voted in favour of responsible government. On 12 Sept. 1923 the country was formally annexed to HM Dominions, and on 1 Oct. 1923 government was established under a Governor, assisted by an Executive Council and a legislature, with the status of a self-governing colony.

By an Order in Council dated 6 Dec. 1961, Southern Rhodesia was granted the new Constitution. Under this the Legislative Assembly consists of 65 Members–50 on the Upper Roll and 15 on the Lower Roll, thus ensuring African representation. Most of the reserved rights of the UK were replaced by a Declaration of Rights, a Constitutional Council and other safeguards.

After the dissolution of the Federation of Rhodesia and Nyasaland on 31 Dec. 1963, Southern Rhodesia reverted to the status of a self-governing colony within the Commonwealth, but, at the same time, became responsible for those powers which had been surrendered to the Federal Government on its formation and which, once again, became its responsibility. These included agriculture (European), defence, education (non-African), external affairs, health services, taxation and other fiscal responsibilities, posts. trade, transport and power.

Ian Smith, Prime Minister from 14 Apr. 1964, had, in London, discussions about independence with the Prime Ministers, Sir Alec Douglas-Home (7–8 Sept. 1964) and Harold Wilson (4–11 Oct. 1965); and in Salisbury with the Prime Minister Wilson, the Commonwealth Secretary and the Attorney-General (25–30 Oct. 1965).

On 5 Nov. 1965 Prime Minister Smith declared a state of emergency, overriding normal constitutional safeguards. After abortive appeals by Prime Minister Wilson (10–11 Nov.), the Smith Government issued a unilateral Declaration of Independence on 11 Nov. 1965. Thereupon the Governor dismissed Prime Minister Smith and his Cabinet. The British Government reasserted its own formal responsibility for Rhodesia, excluded Rhodesia from Commonwealth preference in trade and from the sterling area, and had an enabling Bill passed by Parliament on 15 Nov. which gave the Government power to deal with the situation by Orders in Council. Effective internal government was nevertheless carried on by the Smith Cabinet.

On 20 Nov. the United Nations Security Council called upon all member states to break off economic relations with Rhodesia. Only Portugal and the Republic of South Africa did not impose an embargo, which from 17 Dec. also included oil.

In Sept. 1966 the conference of the Commonwealth Prime Ministers urged the British Government to approach the United Nations with a view to imposing mandatory selective sanctions, unless Rhodesia returned to legality by the end of 1966. From 1 to 3 Dec. Prime Minister Wilson, the Commonwealth Secretary, the Attorney-General, the Governor and the Chief Justice of Rhodesia met Mr Smith and a colleague on board HMS *Tiger*. They drafted a 'Working Document' on the procedure for progress towards legal independence on the basis of the 1961 Constitution and the so-called 'six principles'. This statement was approved by the British Cabinet on 4 Dec., but rejected by the Smith Government on 5 Dec. As a result the British Government approached the United Nations and on 16 Dec. 1966 the Security Council voted for mandatory sanctions including oil; France and USSR abstained.

Further talks based on the *Tiger* proposals were held between the British and Rhodesian Prime Ministers aboard HMS *Fearless* at Gibraltar on 10–13 Oct. 1968. On 2 Mar. 1970 the Smith régime declared Rhodesia a republic and adopted a new Constitution. A general election was held on 10 Apr. 1970. The Rhodesian Front Party won 50 of the 66 seats. On 28 May the first Republican Parliament was opened by the President.

The British Government stated, on 3 March 1970, that 'The purported assumption of a republican status by the régime in Southern Rhodesia is, like the 1965 declaration of independence itself, illegal.'

On 24 Nov. 1971 an agreement was signed between Britain and Rhodesia, following an announcement made on 8 Oct. 1970 that Britain would attempt further negotiations. The terms of the agreement of British recognition of the independence of Rhodesia included the principle that the British Government would need to be satisfied that any basis proposed for independence was acceptable to the people of Rhodesia as a whole. On 11 Jan. 1972 a Commission under Lord Pearce arrived in Rhodesia to carry out a test of acceptability. On 23 May 1972 the report of the Commission found that the proposals were not acceptable to the people of Rhodesia as a whole.

Under the Republican Constitution of Nov. 1969, legislative authority is exercised by the President and a bicameral Parliament. The Senate has 23 Members. Three Senators are nominated by the President, 10 European

Members are elected by the European Members of the House of Assembly, and 5 African Chiefs, elected by Members of the Council of Chiefs from Matabeleland, and 5 from Mashonaland. The House of Assembly has 66 Members including 50 Europeans and 16 Africans. The 50 European Members are elected from a roll of European voters and 8 African Members from a roll of African voters, whilst the remaining 8 African Members are elected by African Electoral Colleges.

ROMANIA

The legislature is the Grand National Assembly (*Marea Adunăre Naţională*) of 465 Deputies elected for constituencies with equal numbers of voters, by all citizens over 18 years in universal, equal, secret and direct elections, for a 5-year term. Deputies must be at least 23 years. The Communist Party, trade unions, co-operatives, youth organisations, women's organisations, cultural organisations and other recognised public institutions may put up candidates. Electoral law provides for the nomination of one or more candidates for each constituency.

Elections to the Grand National Assembly are held on 1 non-working day in the last month of the previous legislature. The date of elections must be set at least 60 days in advance. The newly-elected Grand National Assembly is convened not less than 3 months after the expiry of the previous Grand National Assembly's term of office. The Grand National Assembly's mandate cannot cease until the term it has been elected for expires. It may, however, prolong its term if there are deemed to be circumstances which make it impossible to hold elections.

The Grand National Assembly elects a Bureau, consisting of the Chairman of the Grand National Assembly and 4 Vice-Chairmen. It elects specialised standing Commissions which report on Bills or other matters sent for them to study, and may also elect *ad hoc* Commissions as it deems necessary. Being charged with the observance of the constitutionality of laws, it also elects a Constitutional Commission, which may be one-third comprised of experts who are not Deputies.

The Grand National Assembly adopts and amends the Constitution, regulates the electoral system, ratifies and denounces international treaties, and elects, recalls and supervises the activities of the State Council and the Council of Ministers.

The State Council consists of a President, 4 Vice-Presidents, 1 Secretary and 20 Members.

The State Council is the supreme organ of state power between the sessions of the Grand National Assembly, which are convened by it for 2 approximately fortnightly sessions per year. Extraordinary sessions of the Grand National Assembly may be convened by the State Council or by at least two-thirds of the Deputies.

The State Council establishes norms with the force of law, so long as these do not contravene the Constitution. These norms must be tabled for debate at the next session of the Grand National Assembly. The State Council also gives laws in force a general and compulsory application, and may issue decrees with the force of law.

The quorum of the Grand National Assembly is half the total number of Deputies plus 1. Bills become law upon a majority vote of the total number of Deputies. Bills to amend the Constitution require the vote of two-thirds of all Deputies. Laws are published in *Buletinul oficial*.

Deputies have the right to put questions or address interpellations to Ministers, who are obliged to reply within a maximum of 3 days.

RWANDA

Legislative power was exercised by a National Assembly (*Assemblée Nationale*). The 47 Members were elected by universal adult suffrage for a 4-year term. Following a military *coup* on 5 July 1973 the National Assembly was suspended.

ST HELENA

St Helena is administered by a Governor, with the aid of a Legislative Council consisting of the Governor, 2 *ex-officio* Members (the Government Secretary and the Treasurer) and 12 elected Members. Committees of the Legislative Council are responsible for the general oversight of the activities of government departments and have, in addition, statutory and administrative functions.

SAN MARINO

The present Constitution is based on statutes dating back to 1600 A.D. One of the most important reforms of modern times was introduced in Mar. 1906 when universal male suffrage was introduced, and this system of popular election replaced that of co-option by the Great and General Council (Parliament). This Council, together with The *Arengo,* the Captains-Regent, the State Council (Cabinet) and the Council of XII, constitute the five principal organs of government.

The *Arengo* comprises the general meeting of all heads of families and exercises the supreme legislative power of the community. However, for centuries the *Arengo* has delegated this power to the Great and General Council (but reserving to itself absolutely the right to make decisions concerning changes in the Statutes), so that today the *Arengo* and the Great and General Council are virtually the same electoral body, made up of all citizens of 21 years who are in possession of full civil and political rights. Nevertheless, the *Arengo,* as such, is still the final repository of sovereignty and is still convened twice a year as a symbol of the perpetuation of its powers.

The Great and General Council is formed of 60 elected Members, presided over by the Captains-Regent. From about 1500–1906 A.D. the Councillors were appointed for life, but in Mar. 1906 male citizens were given the right to vote and the Council became elective. The Council is elected for a 4-year term. Women were given the franchise in 1959 and in 1974 became eligible to stand as candidates. To be eligible for election to the Council, the full age of 25 years must have been attained.

The Council exercises the legislative power conferred upon it by the *Arengo.* It makes all laws and elects the Captains-Regent.

SAUDI ARABIA

The Kingdom has been welded together from Hejaz, Nejd, Asir and Al-Hassa. In 1958 a 'Cabinet system' was instituted under which, from 1962, effective power devolved upon the President of the Council of Ministers. The Constitution also provides for the setting up of certain advisory councils, comprising a consultative Legislative Assembly in Mecca, municipal councils in each of the towns of Mecca, Medina and Jidda, and village and tribal councils throughout the provinces. The Members of these councils consist of chief officials and of notables nominated or approved of by the King.

SENEGAL

Legislative power is exercised by the unicameral National Assembly consisting of 100 Members elected for a 5-year term. Senegal is a one-party state. The Assembly debates Bills and submits them to the President. The President can insist that a second reading of a Bill be given, in which case a three-fifths majority is required. The Supreme Court can also give opinions on the constitutional aspects and acceptability of any Bill. Legislation can be initiated by the President or the National Assembly.

SEYCHELLES

A new Constitution was introduced in 1970. The Legislative Assembly consists of 15 elected Members, 3 *ex-officio* Members and a Speaker.

SIERRA LEONE

The House of Representatives has 85 Members elected by direct universal suffrage, and 12 paramount Chiefs.

SIKKIM

The *Chogyal* (Divinely appointed King) governed Sikkim with the help of the Sikkim Council, consisting of 18 elected Members, 7 seats being reserved for Bhutias and Lepchas, 7 seats for Nepalis, 1 seat for Tsongs, 1 seat for Sangha (the monasteries), 1 seat for the scheduled castes and 1 for general interests, and 6 Members nominated by the *Chogyal*. Political reforms were demanded by the National Congress and the Janta Congress in 1973 and elections took place for a Sikkim Assembly in April, 1973, and these were the first elections to be held on the basis of 'one man, one vote'. In May 1974 all effective power was transferred to an Indian Chief Executive. A Council of Ministers was established, responsible to the Assembly and the *Chogyal* was reduced to a titular Head of State.

REPUBLIC OF SINGAPORE

The legislature of Singapore consists of the President of the Republic and Parliament. Laws in and for Singapore are enacted by the President with the advice and consent of Parliament.

The President is elected by Parliament from among the citizens of Singapore and from the date he takes office he presides for a 4-year term.

Parliament consists of 65 Members elected by secret ballot in single-member constituencies and continues for 5 years from the date of its first sitting, unless it is dissolved sooner. A general election follows within 3 months after a dissolution. The commencement of sessions, prorogation and dissolution of Parliament and the holding of a general election, are appointed by the President.

Every citizen of Singapore of 21 years and over may be elected as a Member of Parliament subject to certain qualifications: if his name appears in a current register of electors; if he is resident in Singapore at the date of his nomination for election; if he is able, with a degree of proficiency sufficient to enable him to take an active part in the proceedings of Parliament, to speak and, unless incapacitated by blindness or other physical cause, to read and write at least one of the following languages, namely, Malay, Mandarin, Tamil and English.

Any citizen of Singapore of 21 years or over is entitled to have his name entered or retained in a register of electors. Voting at an election is compulsory.

Parliament is presided over by the Speaker, who is elected by Parliament either from among the Members of Parliament who are neither Ministers nor Parliamentary Secretaries, or from among persons who are not Members but who are qualified for election as Members. A Speaker who is elected from among Members has an original, but no casting, vote. If he is elected from among persons who are not Members, he has no right to vote.

Parliament meets periodically but there are no scheduled dates of sittings, which are held in Parliament House and are open to the public. In debates Members may speak in Malay, Mandarin, Tamil or English and simultaneous translations are provided.

The Member of Parliament who can command the confidence of the majority of the Members of Parliament is appointed Prime Minister by the President. On the advice of the Prime Minister the President also appoints from among Members of Parliament the Ministers who form the Cabinet. One Cabinet Minister also fills the post of Deputy Prime Minister.

SOLOMON ISLANDS

Under the 1970 Constitution a unicameral Governing Council was created. There are 17 elected and 3 *ex-officio* Members meeting three times a year in public legislative session.

SOMALI DEMOCRATIC REPUBLIC

The Constitution of the Somali Republic was established under the Italian trusteeship, during 1960. The two regions provisionally adopted it in July 1960 by means of an Act of Union, and it was approved by a national referendum in June 1961. The Somali armed forces took over supreme power in the country from the civilian Government in Oct. 1969. The Parliament (*Parlamanka*) was dismissed, the Constitution was suspended and the Supreme Court dissolved. A Supreme Revolutionary Council was formed which took over the responsibility of legislature, executive and judiciary.

REPUBLIC OF SOUTH AFRICA

Legislative power is vested in a Parliament (*Parlement*) consisting of the State President, a Senate (*Senaat*) and a House of Assembly (*Volksraad*). The State President has power to summon, prorogue and dissolve Parliament, either both Houses simultaneously or the House of Assembly alone. He may also dissolve the Senate at any time within 120 days of any dissolution of the House of Assembly, or the expiry of the term of office of a provincial council. A session of Parliament must be held once at least in every year.

The Senate consists of 54 Members, 10 being nominated by the State President in Council (2 for each of the Provinces and 2 for South West Africa) and 44 being elected by electoral colleges (15 in the Transvaal, 11 in the Cape Province, 8 in Natal, 8 in the Orange Free State, 2 in South West Africa). An electoral college consists of the Members of Parliament and of the Provincial Council of the province concerned. In South West Africa, the electoral college is made up of the members of Parliament and the members of the Legislative Assembly of South West Africa. A Senator must be a white South African citizen, at least 30 years of age, qualified as a voter in one of the provinces and resident for 5 years within the Republic. Senators hold their seats for 5 years, subject to a prior dissolution of the Senate.

At least one of the 2 Senators nominated by the State President from each province should be thoroughly acquainted with the interests of the coloured population. Similarly, one of the Senators nominated from South West Africa should be selected mainly for his thorough acquaintance with the reasonable wants and wishes of the coloured races of the Territory.

The House of Assembly consists of 171 Members until 1983. They are chosen in electoral divisions as follows: Cape of Good Hope, 55; Natal, 20; Transvaal, 76; Orange Free State, 14; South West Africa, 6.

A Member of the House of Assembly must be a white South African citizen, qualified as a voter and resident for 5 years within the Republic. Every House of Assembly continues for 5 years, unless dissolved sooner. Adult suffrage is at 18 years for white citizens.

Only the House of Assembly can originate money Bills, but may not pass a Bill for taxation or appropriation unless it has been recommended by the State President during the session. Restrictions are placed on the amendment of money Bills by the Senate. Provision is made respecting disagreements between the Houses and the State President's assent to Bills.

A Member of one House cannot be elected to the other, but a Minister and a Deputy Minister may sit and speak, but not vote, in the House of which he is not a Member. To hold an office of profit under the State (with certain exceptions) is a disqualification for membership of either House, as are also insolvency, crime and insanity. Pretoria is the seat of government, and Cape Town is the seat of legislature.

South West Africa (Namibia)

The territory (excluding Walvis Bay and certain islands) was proclaimed a German protectorate in 1884, but was surrendered to the forces of the Union of South Africa on 9 July 1915 at Khorab. The administration was vested in the Government of the Union of South Africa by mandate of the League of Nations, dated 17 Dec. 1920. In 1921 the Governor-General delegated certain of his functions to the Administrator of the Territory, who was assisted by an Advisory Council and, from 1925, by an Executive Committee and the Legislative Assembly. In 1971 the International Court of Justice ruled, in an advisory opinion, that the presence of South Africa in Namibia was illegal.

The South West Africa Affairs Amendment Act, 1949, abolished the Advisory Council and the nominated Members of the Legislative Assembly. All 18 Members of the Assembly are now elected by the registered voters of the territory. The territory is represented in the South African House of Assembly by 6 Members elected by the registered voters of the territory, and in the Senate by 4 Senators, of which number 2 are elected by the Members of the Legislative Assembly and the representatives of the territory in the House of Assembly, and 2 nominated by the President of the Republic. One of the nominated Senators is selected mainly on the ground of his acquaintance with the conditions of the coloured races of South West Africa.

On 13 Oct. 1966 the security and apartheid laws of the Republic of South Africa were extended to South West Africa, retrospective to 1950. On 2 Oct. 1968 the South African Government announced the formation of a 42-member Legislative Council for Ovamboland.

A Commission of Inquiry, appointed by the South African Government, in 1964 recommended the establishment of 'homeland areas' for the non-White groups. It further suggested that all these areas should be governed by Legislative Councils, headed by executive committees; franchise should be granted to males and females over 18 years who qualify for citizenship in their respective homelands.

On 17 Oct. 1968 and 22 Oct. 1970 respectively, the first sessions of the Legislative Councils of Ovambo (42 Members) and Kavango (30 Members) were opened.

SOUTHERN YEMEN (PEOPLE'S DEMOCRATIC REPUBLIC OF YEMEN)

Pending the appointment or election of a permanent Council, the 101-member Provisional Supreme People's Council exercises legislative authority. A new Constitution came into force on 30 Nov. 1970. Every citizen of 18 years or over may vote for the People's Councils and may be elected at 21 years. The People's Supreme Council of 101 Members is the legislative authority.

SPAIN

The Organic Law distinguishes the executive powers of the Head of State (*Jefe del Estado*) and those of a Premier (*Presidente del Gobierno*), who is to be chosen by the Head of State from a list of 3 names submitted by the Council of the Realm; the Premier is chosen for a 5-year term though he may be removed earlier by the Head of State on the proposal of the Council of the Realm, but not by the *Cortes*.

'The Head of the State directs the government apparatus (*gobernación*) of the Kingdom by means of the Council of Ministers.... In the absence or illness of the Chief of State, his functions will be assumed by the Heir to the Throne if over 30 years, or by the Council of Regency'.

The Council of the Realm consists of 16 Members, 10 of them elected by the *Cortes*; the President of the *Cortes* is its chairman.

The National Council consists of 1 elected Councillor for each province, 40 Councillors appointed by the Head of State, 12 Councillors elected by the *Cortes* to represent 'basic structures of the nation' (family, local corporations, trade unions), 6 Councillors appointed by the Prime Minister and a Secretary-General appointed by the Head of State.

The *Cortes* are composed of the members of the Government; the national Councillors; the Presidents of the Supreme Court of Justice, the Council of the Realm, the Supreme Military Tribunal, the Court of Exchequer and the National Economic Council; 150 representatives of the trade unions; representatives of the municipalities and provincial councils elected by their respective corporations; 100 Deputies (2 from each province) elected by the heads of families (men or women); and some 30 representatives of the universities, learned and professional societies, Chambers of Commerce, etc. The maximum term of office between elections is 4 years.

SRI LANKA (CEYLON)

Parliament is unicameral consisting of a National State Assembly. There are 157 Members, of these 151 are elected by universal suffrage by citizens over 18 years for a 6-year term, and 6 Members are nominated. From 1977 all Members of the Assembly will be elected.

THE DEMOCRATIC REPUBLIC OF THE SUDAN

In May 1973 a permanent Constitution came into force. The first elections to the National Assembly under the new Constitution were held for the 125 elective seats in May 1974. The remaining 125 seats were for nominated Members.

SWAZILAND

On 12 Apr. 1973 King Sobhuza II took over the supreme legislative power. The processes of introducing Bills and enacting Laws is performed through a Council of Ministers. The Parliament, which was bicameral, consisted of a House of Assembly, with 24 elected and 6 nominated Members; the Attorney-General, who had no vote; and a Senate comprising 12 Members, 6 of whom were elected by the House of Assembly and 6 appointed by the King. There is universal adult suffrage at 21 years.

SWEDEN

The Diet (*Riksdag*) is unicameral. Until 1970 the Diet was bicameral. The Diet consists of 350 Members elected for 3-year terms. All citizens who have reached 19 years not later than the calendar year preceding election year may vote and stand for election as a Member. Election to the Diet is proportional. Sweden is divided into 28 constituencies. In these constituencies 310 Members are elected. The remaining 40 seats constitute a nationwide pool intended to give absolute proportionality to parties that receive at least 4 per cent of the votes. A party receiving less than 4 per cent of the votes in the country is, however, entitled to participate in the distribution of seats in a constituency if it has obtained at least 12 per cent of the votes cast there.

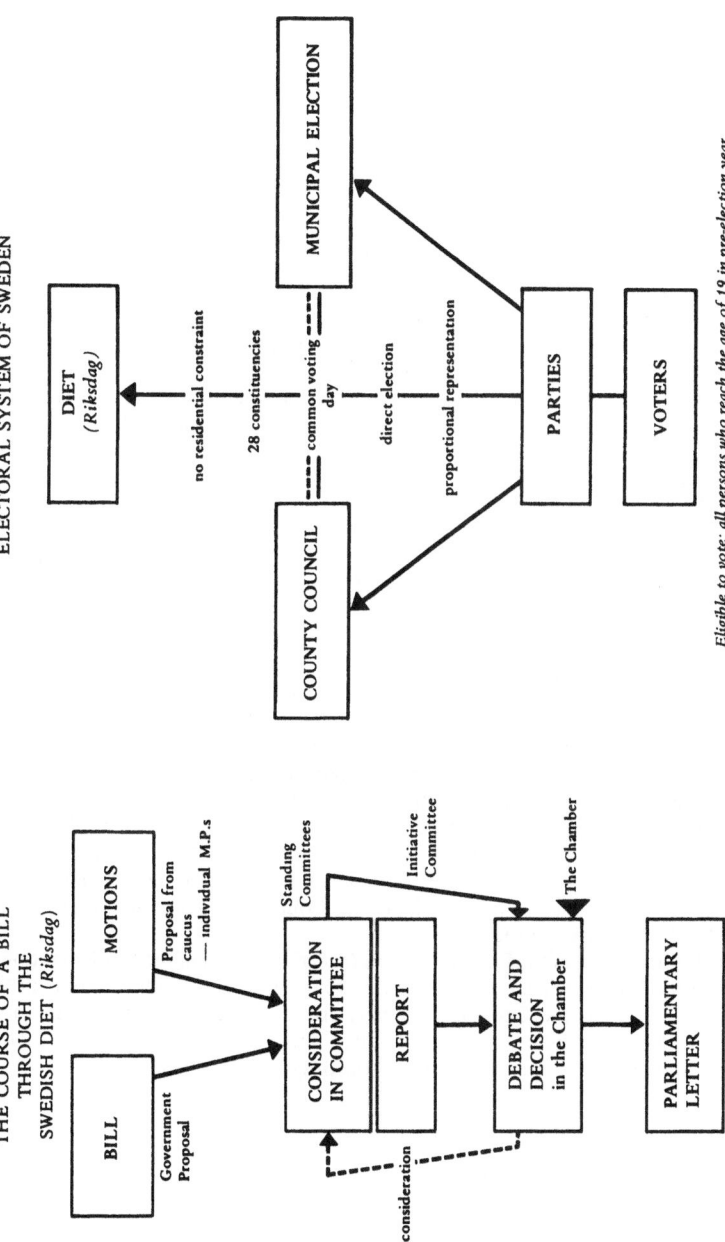

ELECTORAL SYSTEM OF SWEDEN

DIET (*Riksdag*)

no residential constraint

28 constituencies

common voting day

direct election

proportional representation

MUNICIPAL ELECTION

COUNTY COUNCIL

PARTIES

VOTERS

Eligible to vote: all persons who reach the age of 19 in pre-election year.

THE COURSE OF A BILL THROUGH THE SWEDISH DIET (*Riksdag*)

MOTIONS

Proposal from caucus — individual M.P.s

BILL

Government Proposal

Standing Committees

CONSIDERATION IN COMMITTEE

Initiative Committee

REPORT

The Chamber

DEBATE AND DECISION in the Chamber

PARLIAMENTARY LETTER

Reconsideration

SWITZERLAND

The legislative authority is vested in a bicameral Parliament. This consists of a Council of States (*Standerat*) and a National Council (*Nationalrat*). The *Standerat* is composed of 44 Members, chosen and paid by the 22 cantons of the Confederation, 2 for each canton. The mode of their election and the term of membership depend entirely on the canton. Three of the cantons are politically divided–Basel into Stadt and Land, Appenzell into Ausser-Rhoden and Inner-Rhoden, and Unterwalden into Obwalden and Nidwalden. Each of these 'half-cantons' sends one Member to the State Council.

The *Nationalrat* consists of 200 National Councillors, directly elected for 4 years, in proportion to the population of the cantons, with the proviso that each canton or half-canton is represented by at least 1 Member. A general election takes place by ballot every 4 years. Every citizen of the Republic who is over 20 years is entitled to a vote, and any voter, not a clergyman, may be elected a Deputy. Laws passed by both Chambers may be submitted to direct popular vote, when 30,000 citizens or 8 cantons demand it; the vote can be only 'Yes' or 'No'. This principle, called the 'referendum', is frequently acted on.

Women's suffrage, although advocated by the Federal Council and the Federal Assembly, was rejected on 1 Feb. 1959 but in a subsequent referendum, held on 7 Feb. 1971, women's suffrage was carried.

The chief executive authority is deputed to the *Bundesrat*, or Federal Council, consisting of 7 Members, elected from 7 different cantons for 4 years by the *Vereinigte Bundesversammlung, i.e.*, joint session of both Chambers. The Members of this council must not hold any other office in the Confederation or cantons; nor engage in any calling or business. In the Federal Parliament legislation may be introduced either by a Member, or by either House, or by the Federal Council (but not by the people). Every citizen who has a vote for the National Council is eligible for becoming a Member of the executive.

The President of the Federal Council (called President of the Confederation) and the Vice-President, are the first magistrates of the Confederation. Both are elected by the Federal Assembly for 1 calendar year and are not immediately re-eligible to the same offices. The Vice-President, however, may be, and usually is, elected to succeed the outgoing President.

SYRIA

A People's Council (*Majlis esh-Sháb*) with a 2-year term appointed in 1971. This was the first legislative authority since 1966, when the National Assembly was dissolved. In 1973 the People's Council of 128 Members was elected by adult (at 18 years) universal suffrage for a period of 4 years. There are 6 women Members.

TAIWAN (REPUBLIC OF CHINA)

The National Assembly (*Kuo-min Ta-hui*) has 1,376 Members (mainly former Members of mainland constituencies) and 53 Members elected by universal adult suffrage. The highest legislative organ is the Legislative *yuan* (governing body) and consists of elected Members.

TANZANIA

In 1964 Tanganyika, Zanzibar and Pemba combined to form the United Republic of Tanganyika, later named Tanzania. The National Assembly (*Bunge*) is composed of 120 elected Members from the mainland, 10 Members appointed from both Tanganyika and Zanzibar, 15 National Members (elected by the National Assembly after nomination by various national institutions), 20 Regional Commissioners, up to 32 Members of the Zanzibar Revolutionary Council and up to 20 other Zanzibar Members appointed by the President in agreement with the President of Zanzibar.

THAILAND

The interim Constitution of 1972 provides for a unicameral National Legislative Assembly (*Sapaa Niti Banyat*) of 299 Members; 200 Members from armed services and police, and 99 civilians, appointed by the King for a 3-year term. Members must be Thai nationals and over 35 years. One third of all Members present in the Assembly represent a quorum. A new Constitution was drafted in 1974 which would provide for a House of Representations of 240–300 Members elected for a 4-year term by universal suffrage. Minimum voting age would be 18 years.

TOGO

Since 1967 the Constitution and the 56-member National Assembly have been suspended. A Constitutional Committee completed the draft of a new Constitution in 1969.

TONGA

The present Constitution is almost identical with that granted in 1875 by King George Tupou I. There is a Privy Council, Cabinet, Legislative Assembly and Judiciary. The Legislative Assembly, which meets annually, is composed of 7 nobles elected by their peers, 7 elected representatives of the people and the Privy Councillors (numbering 8); the King appoints one of the 7 nobles to be the Speaker. The Legislative Assembly has a 3-year term. The franchise is for all Tongans over 21 years.

TRINIDAD AND TOBAGO

The Constitution provides for a bicameral legislature of a Senate and a House of Representatives. The Senate consists of 24 Members appointed by the Governor-General, 13 of them on the advice of the Prime Minister, 4 on the advice of the Leader of the Opposition and 7 from religious, economic and social bodies which the Prime Minister considers should be represented. The House of Representatives consists of 36 elected Members.

TUNISIA

The Constitution of the Republic was promulgated on 1 June 1959. The President and the National Assembly (*Majlis el-Umma*) are elected simultaneously by direct universal suffrage for a 5-year term. All who have had Tunisian nationality for 5 years, and are over 20 years, may vote.

TURKEY

The Grand National Assembly (*Türkiye Büyük Millet Meclisi*) is bicameral and consists of the National Assembly (*Millet Meclisi*) and the Senate (*Cumhuriyet Senatosu*). The National Assembly has 450 Members elected for a 4-year term by direct general ballot. The Senate has 150 Members elected by direct general ballot and the President nominates 15 Members. The President is elected by the National Assembly and the Senate in joint session for a 7-year term. Turkish citizens are entitled to vote at the age of 21 years and to become Deputies at the age of 30 years.

TURKS AND CAICOS ISLANDS

The Constitution provides for an Administrator and a State Council. The State Council consists of a Speaker, 3 official Members, not less than 2 or more than 3 nominated Members, and 9 elected Members. Normally the State Council has a 5-year term.

UGANDA

Under the 1967 Constitution a unicameral Parliament is the supreme legislature and consists of a President and a National Assembly. The Assembly has 82 elected Members. Although the Constitution is still in existence the President ordered the suspension of the legal system in 1971 and that legislative power be exercised by the President and a nominated Council of Ministers.

UNION OF SOVIET SOCIALIST REPUBLICS

The Soviet Union is a socialist state of workers and peasants, the political units of which are the soviets of Working People's Deputies. All central and local authority is vested in these Soviets.

The Constitution recognises the right of all citizens to work, rest, leisure, education and maintenance in old age, sickness or incapacity, without distinction of sex, race or nationality, and lays down that any direct or indirect restriction of the rights of, or conversely, the establishment of direct or indirect privileges for, citizens on account of their race or nationality, as well as the advocacy of racial or national exclusiveness or hatred and contempt, is punishable by law. The franchise is enjoyed by all citizens of the USSR, including members of the armed forces, who have reached the age of 18 years, irrespective of sex, with the exception of the insane and of persons convicted by a court of law to sentences including deprivation of rights. Candidates for election to the Supreme Soviet of the USSR must be 23 years, and to the supreme soviets of the union republics and autonomous republics 21 years; for all regional and other local authorities the minimum age for candidates is 18 years. A Member of any soviet may be recalled by a decision of a majority of his or her electors if he or she fails to give satisfaction.

The USSR consists of 15 union republics, each inhabited by a major nationality which gives its name to the republic.

The highest legislative organ is the Supreme Soviet of the USSR. It consists of 2 Chambers with equal legislative rights, elected for a 4-year term: the Soviet of the Union and the Soviet of Nationalities.

The Soviet of the Union is elected by the citizens of the USSR on the basis of 1 Deputy for every 300,000 of the population. The Chamber had 767 Members in 1970.

The Soviet of Nationalities is elected by the citizens of the USSR, voting by union and autonomous republics, autonomous regions and national areas, on the basis of 32 Deputies from each union Republic, 11 Deputies from each autonomous republic, 5 Deputies from each autonomous region and 1 Deputy from each national area. The Chamber had 750 Members in 1970.

Each Chamber has 12 Standing Committees: planning and budget; industry; transport and communications; building; agriculture; health and social welfare; education, science and culture; trade and services; draft legislation; foreign affairs; youth affairs; natural environment.

The highest executive and administrative organ is the Council of Ministers (called People's Commissars before 16 Mar. 1946); they are appointed by the Supreme Soviet.

The Presidium of the Supreme Soviet of the USSR is elected at a joint session of both Chambers of the Supreme Soviet and consists of the Chairman, 15 Vice-Chairmen (one from each of the Union Republics), 20 Members and the Secretary. It acts as the supreme state authority between sessions of the Supreme Soviet and is accountable to the latter for all its activities.

Deputies are elected by the voters on the basis of universal, equal and direct suffrage by secret ballot. The only legal political party is the Communist Party; non-members are classed as non-party citizens. Up to the present candidates have been selected at a preliminary 'constituency electoral consultation' (selection conference), to which organisations which have put forward nominations send Delegates, who discuss the various nominees. As a consequence so far, a single candidate has been arrived at in each constituency, whose name has appeared on the ballot paper to be struck out or approved by a cross as the voter desires. This procedure, however, is not laid down by the Constitution, and may be altered. The Supreme Soviet elected in 1970 consists of 1,096 Communist and 421 non-party Deputies; 463 were women, 481 manual workers in industry and state farms, and 282 collective farmers.

On 1 Feb. 1944 each of the constituent republics of the Union was given the right to have separate Commissariats (now Ministries) for defence and foreign affairs. After the death of Stalin, 5 Mar. 1953, a number of ministries comprising different branches of trade, engineering, transport and electricity were merged into single ministries. In 1957 the number of ministries in the central Government was reduced from 52 to 19, and in Dec. 1959 to 15; but in Oct. 1964 it was again increased to 47, in Aug. 1966 to 48 and in 1968 to 56.

The Council of Ministers, in Feb. 1973, included 10 Vice-Chairmen;

the Premiers of the 15 union republics; the head of the Central Statistical Department; the Chairmen of 7 commissions of the Presidium of the Council of Ministers (4 of them Vice-Chairmen of the Council), of the Committee for People's Control, State Planning Committee, the Agricultural Technique Organisation and of 7 other state committees; 58 Ministers; and the Chairman of the State Bank.

Soon after the adoption of the 1936 Constitution all the constituent republics of the Union held their soviet congresses, at which they adopted their own Constitutions based in all essentials on the Constitution of the Union, but adapted, where necessary, to national and local requirements. Article 14 of the Constitution reserves to the central Government the spheres of war and peace, diplomatic relations, defence, foreign trade, state security, economic planning, education, criminal and civil codes, etc. The right of the constituent republics to withdraw from the Union is expressly recognised.

The autonomous republics are governed by their own Supreme Soviet and Council of Ministers: the regions and territories, districts, towns and rural areas have their own soviets, elected for a 2-year term.

In Nov. 1970 there were over 44,000 rural and urban soviets with 1·5 m. Deputies, 1·7 m. voluntary co-opted Members participating in their standing committees, and 43,000 women were chairmen or secretaries of soviets.

Armenia

The Supreme Soviet elected in 1971 consisted of 310 Deputies (1 for every 5,000 of population) of which 103 were women; 205 were Communists.

Azerbaijan

The Supreme Soviet elected in 1971 consisted of 385 Deputies (1 for every 10,000 of population) of which 142 were women; 269 were Communists.

Belorussia

The Supreme Soviet elected in 1971 consisted of 425 Deputies (1 for every 20,000 of population) of which 157 were women; 296 were Communists.

Estonia

The Supreme Soviet elected in 1971 consisted of 183 Deputies (1 for every 10,000 of population) of which 61 were women; 122 were Communists.

Georgia

The Supreme Soviet elected in 1971 consisted of 400 Deputies (1 for every 10,000 of population) of which 141 were women; 264 were Communists.

Kazakhstan

The Supreme Soviet elected in 1971 consisted of 482 Deputies (1 for every 20,000 of population) of which 170 were women; 319 were Communists.

Kirghizia

The Supreme Soviet elected in 1971 consisted of 339 Deputies (1 for every 5,000 of population) of which 120 were women; 231 were Communists.

Latvia

The Supreme Soviet elected in 1971 consisted of 310 Deputies (1 for every 10,000 of population) of which 106 were women; 202 were Communists.

Lithuania

The Supreme Soviet elected in 1971 consisted of 300 Deputies (1 for every 15,000 of population) of which 97 were women; 203 were Communists.

Moldavia

The Supreme Soviet elected in 1971 consisted of 315 Deputies (1 for every 10,000 of population) of which 113 were women; 210 were Communists.

Russia

The Supreme Soviet elected in 1971 consisted of 894 Deputies (1 for every 150,000 of population) of which 309 were women; 597 were Communists.

Tadzhikstan

The Supreme Soviet elected in 1971 consisted of 315 Deputies (1 for every 5,000 of population) of which 107 were women; 217 were Communists.

Turkmenistan

The Supreme Soviet elected in 1971 consisted of 285 Deputies (1 for every 5,000 of population) of which 100 were women; 193 were Communists.

Ukraine

The Supreme Soviet elected in 1971 consisted of 484 Deputies (1 for every 90,000 of population) of which 168 were women; 385 were Communists.

Uzbekistan

The Supreme Soviet elected in 1971 consisted of 452 Deputies (1 for every 15,000 of population) of which 151 were women; 311 were Communists.

UNITED ARAB EMIRATES

British forces withdrew from the Gulf at the end of 1971 and the treaties whereby Britain had been responsible for the defence and foreign relations of the Trucial States were terminated, being replaced in Dec. 1971 by a treaty of friendship between Britain and the United Arab Emirates. The United Arab Emirates (formed Dec. 1971) consists of the former Trucial States: Abu Dhabi, Dubai, Sharjah, Ajman, Umm al Qaiwain, Ras el Khaimah (joined in Feb. 1972) and Fujairah. The small state of Kalba was merged with Sharjah in 1952. The ruler of Abu Dhabi has a Cabinet and a National Consultative Assembly. Other rulers have absolute control over their subjects. A Provisional Constitution was published in 1973 which envisaged a National Assembly of the Union.

UNITED KINGDOM

Legislative power is vested in Parliament, which is divided into two Houses of legislature.

Parliament is summoned by the writ of the Sovereign issued out of Chancery, by advice of the Privy Council, at least 20 days previous to its assembling. Every session must end with a prorogation, and all Bills which have not been passed during the session then lapse. A dissolution may occur by the will of the Sovereign, or, as is most usual during the recess, by proclamation, or finally by lapse of time. The statury limit of the duration of any Parliament is 5 years.

Under the Parliament Acts, 1911 (1 and 2 Geo.V, ch. 13) and 1949 (12, 13 and 24 Geo.VI, ch. 103), all money Bills (so certified by the Speaker of the House of Commons), if not passed by the House of Lords without amendment, may become law without their concurrence, on the royal assent being signified. Public Bills, other than money Bills or a Bill extending the maximum duration of Parliament, if passed by the House of Commons in 2 successive sessions, whether of the same Parliament or not, and rejected each time, or not passed, by the House of Lords, may become law without their concurrence on the royal assent being signified, provided that 1 year has elapsed between the second reading in the first session of the House of Commons and the third reading in the second session. All Bills coming under this Act must reach the House of Lords at least 1 month before the end of the session.

The House of Lords consists of: (1) hereditary peers and peeresses sitting by virtue of creation or descent, other than those who have disclaimed their titles for life under the provisions of the Peerage Act, 1963; (2) life peers being (a) 24 Lords of Appeal (active and retired), under the Appellate Jurisdiction Act, 1876, as amended, (b) (Jan. 1973) 207 life peers and peeresses under the Life Peerages Act, 1958; (3) 2 archbishops and 24 bishops (as long as they hold their sees). The full House consists of about 1,075, of whom about 97 are without a writ of summons, and the average attendance is about 250; in 1972–3, 182 peers were on leave of absence.

The House of Commons consists of Members representing county and borough constituencies. Persons under 21 years, clergymen of the Church of England, ministers of the Church of Scotland, Roman Catholic clergymen, civil servants, members of the regular armed forces, policemen and most judicial officers are disqualified from sitting in the House of Commons. No English or Scottish peer can be elected to the House of Commons unless he has disclaimed his title for life under the Peerage Act, 1963, but Irish peers and holders of courtesy titles are eligible. Under the Parliament (Qualification of Women) Act, 1918, women are also eligible.

In Aug. 1911 provision was first made for the payment of a salary of £400 per annum to Members, other than those already in receipt of salaries as officers of the House, as Ministers or as officers of HM household. As from Oct. 1964 the salaries of Members are £3,250 per annum, with income-tax relief ón expenses incurred in the course of parliamentary duties. A secretarial allowance of £500 came into effect in Oct. 1969. Members of the House of Lords are only entitled to recover expenses incurred for the purpose of attendance at sittings of the House, within a maximum of £6.50 for each day of attendance.

The Representation of the People Act, 1948, abolished the business premises and university franchises, and the only persons entitled to vote at parliamentary elections are those registered as residents or as service voters. No persons may vote in more than one constituency at a general election. Persons may apply on certain grounds to vote by post or by proxy.

All persons over 17 years and not subject to any legal incapacity to vote, and who are either British subjects or citizens of the Irish Republic, are entitled to be included in the register of electors for the constituency containing the address at which they were residing on the qualifying date for the register, and are entitled to vote at elections held during the period for which the register remains in force. The current register was published on 16 Feb. 1973.

Members of the armed forces, Crown servants employed abroad, and the wives accompanying their husbands, are entitled, if otherwise qualified, to be registered as 'service voters' provided they make a 'service declaration'. To be effective for a particular register, the declaration must be made on or before the qualifying date for that register.

The Representation of the People Act, 1969, abolished the occupier's qualification for voting in local government elections.

The Act of 1948 effected a redistribution of the constituencies in the UK. The number of constituencies in Great Britain must be not substantially greater or less than 613, in Scotland not less than 71, in Wales not less than 35 and in Northern Ireland 12. Every constituency returns a single Member.

The House of Commons (Redistribution of Seats) Act, 1944, 1949 and 1958, provided for the setting up of Boundary Commissions for England, Wales, Scotland and Northern Ireland. The Commissions are required to make general reports at intervals of not less than 3, and not more than 7, years and to submit reports from time to time with respect to the area comprised in any particular constituency or constituencies where some change appears necessary. Any changes giving effect to reports of the Commissions are to be made by Orders in Council laid before Parliament for approval by resolution of each House.

The following is a table of the duration of Parliaments called since 1911.

Reign	Assembled	Dissolved	Duration (years and days)	
George V	31 Jan. 1911	25 Nov. 1918	7	301
,,	4 Feb. 1919	26 Oct. 1922	3	269
,,	20 Nov. 1922	16 Nov. 1923	0	362
,,	8 Jan. 1924	9 Oct. 1924	0	276
,,	2 Dec. 1924	10 May 1929	4	161
,,	25 June 1929	7 Oct. 1931	2	75
,,	3 Nov. 1931	25 Oct. 1935	3	358
George V, Edward VIII and George VI	26 Nov. 1935	15 June 1945	9	205
George VI	1 Aug. 1945	3 Feb. 1950	4	188
,,	1 Mar. 1950	5 Oct. 1951	1	219
George VI and Elizabeth II	31 Oct. 1951	6 May 1955	3	188
Elizabeth II	7 June 1955	18 Sept. 1959	4	105
,,	20 Oct. 1959	25 Sept. 1964	4	341
,,	27 Oct. 1964	10 Mar. 1966	1	134
,,	18 Apr. 1966	29 May 1970	4	81
,,	29 June 1970	8 Feb.	3	225
,,	12 Mar. 1974	30 Sept. 1974	—	192

The executive government is vested nominally in the Crown, but practically in a committee of Ministers, called the Cabinet, which is dependent on the support of a majority in the House of Commons.

The head of the Ministry is the Prime Minister, a position first constitutionally recognised, and special precedence accorded to the holder, in 1905.His colleagues in the Ministry are appointed on his recommendation, and he dispenses the greater portion of the patronage of the Crown.

Isle of Man

The Isle of Man is administered in accordance with its own laws by the Court of Tynwald. This consists of the Governor, appointed by the Crown; the Legislative Council, composed of the Lord Bishop of Sodor and Man, the First Deemster, the Attorney-General and 7 Members selected by the House of Keys, (total 11 Members, including the Governor); and the House of Keys, a representative assembly of 24 Members chosen on adult suffrage with 6 months' residence for a 5-year term by the 6 'sheadings' or local sub-divisions, and the 4 municipalities. The island is not bound by Acts of the Imperial Parliament unless specially mentioned in them.

Northern Ireland (Ulster)

The Northern Ireland Assembly was prorogued on 29 May 1974 for a maximum period of 4 months. The Assembly remains in existence during this period but it will not exercise its functions. Legislation which would have been possible in the Assembly will be enacted at Westminster.

The Northern Ireland Constitution Act, 1973, as amended by the Northern Ireland Constitution (Amendment) Act, 1973, provides for a Northern Ireland Executive of not more than 11 Members (including the Chief Executive Member). The Secretary of State appointed this full number to take office from 1 Jan. 1974. He may also, under the Amendment Act, appoint others to carry out particular functions in the Administration up to a total (including Members of the Executive) of 15. This additional number has also been appointed.

Devolution of legislative and executive responsibility to the Northern Ireland Assembly and the new Administration under Section 2 of the Constitution Act was given effect by the Northern Ireland Constitution (Devolution) Order, 1973, from 1 Jan. 1974 ('the Appointed day'). On that day, Section 1 of the Northern Ireland (Temporary Provisions) Act, 1972, expired and, with it, the power to legislate for Northern Ireland by Order in Council under that Act.

Power to make laws (to be known as Measures) in respect of 'transferred' matters, that is, on matters other than those listed in Schedules 2 and 3 to the Constitution Act, is now vested in the Assembly subject to the overriding power of the UK Parliament to legislate on such matters and subject to Section 17 of the Constitution Act which declares void any provision which discriminates against any person or class of persons on the ground of religious belief or political opinion. The procedure for Measures is set out in the Standing Orders of the Assembly. All Measures require the approval of the Queen in Council before they become law. The first election of Members to the 78 seats in the Northern Ireland Assembly was held in 1973. The state of the parties following the election was: Social Democratic and Labour Party 19; Democratic Unionist Loyalist Coalition 8; Official Unionist 24; Northern Ireland Labour 1; Other Unionist 8; Alliance 8; Vanguard Unionist Coalition 7; Other Loyalist Coalition 2; Other Loyalist 1: Northern Ireland also returns 12 Members to the UK House of Commons. The Secretary of State for Northern Ireland maintains an office at Stormont Castle and is supported by a Minister of State and two Parliamentary Under-Secretaries of State.

UNITED STATES OF AMERICA

The legislative power is vested by the Constitution in a Congress, consisting of a Senate and House of Representatives.

By amendments of the Constitution, disqualification of voters on the ground of race, colour or sex is forbidden. Accordingly the electorate consists theoretically of all citizens of both sexes over 18 years, but the franchise is not universal. There are requirements of residence, varying in the several states as to length from 6 months to 2 years, and differing requirements as to registration. In 20 states the ability to read, usually an extract from the Constitution, is required–in Alaska the ability to read English; in Hawaii, English or Hawaiian; in Louisiana, English or one's native tongue. In Alabama the voter must take an 'anti-communist oath' and fill out a questionnaire to the satisfaction of the registrars. In some southern states voters are required to give a reasonable explanation of what they read. In most states convicts are excluded from the franchise and in some states duellists and fraudulent voters are also excluded.

Legislation designed to discourage the rise of third parties has been adopted in a few states. In Illinois a new party must present a petition signed by at least 25,000 voters, including at least 200 in each of 50 of the 102 counties.

The method of balloting varies greatly. Seventeen states use different ballots for federal, state and local elections. In Delaware and South Carolina the various political parties furnish their own ballot papers to the voters as they enter the polling booths.

The Senate consists of 2 Members from each state, chosen by popular vote for 6 years, one-third retiring or seeking re-election every 2 years. Senators must be not less than 30 years; must have been citizens of the USA for 9 years, and be residents in the states for which they are chosen. The Senate has complete freedom to initiate legislation, except revenue Bills (which must originate in the House of Representatives); it may, however, amend or reject any legislation originating in the Lower House. The Senate is also entrusted with the power of giving or withholding its 'advice and consent' to the ratification of all treaties initiated by the President with foreign powers, a two-thirds majority of Senators present being required for approval. (However, it has no control over 'international executive agreements' made by the President with foreign governments; such 'agreements', representing an important but very recent development, cover a wide range and are actually more numerous than formal treaties.) It also has the power of confirming or rejecting major appointments to office made by the President, but it has no direct control over the appointment by the President of 'personal representatives' or 'personal envoys' on missions abroad. Members of the Senate constitute a High Court of Impeachment, with power, by a two-thirds vote, to remove from office and disqualify any civil officer of the USA impeached by the House of Representatives, which has the sole power of impeachment.

The Senate has 16 Standing Committees to which all Bills are referred for study, revision or rejection. The House of Representatives has 21 such committees. In both Houses each Standing Committee has a chairman and a majority representing the majority party of the whole House; each has numerous sub-committees. The jurisdictions of these committees correspond largely to those of the appropriate executive departments and agencies. Both Houses also have a few special committees with limited duration. There are some joint committees of both Houses.

The House of Representatives consists of 435 Members elected every second year. The number of each state's Representatives is determined by the decennial census, in the absence of specific congressional legislation affecting the basis. The states, in 1972, had the following representatives:

Alabama	7	Montana	2
Alaska	1	Nebraska	3
Arizona	4	Nevada	1
Arkansas	4	New Hampshire	2
California	43	New Jersey	15
Colorado	5	New Mexico	2
Connecticut	6	New York	39
Delaware	1	North Carolina	11
Florida	15	North Dakota	1
Georgia	10	Ohio	23
Hawaii	2	Oklahoma	6
Idaho	2	Oregon	4
Illinois	24	Pennsylvania	25
Indiana	11	Rhode Island	2
Iowa	6	South Carolina	6
Kansas	5	South Dakota	2
Kentucky	7	Tennessee	8
Louisiana	8	Texas	24
Maine	2	Utah	2
Maryland	8	Vermont	1
Massachusetts	12	Virginia	10
Michigan	19	Washington	7
Minnesota	8	West Virginia	4
Mississippi	5	Wisconsin	9
Missouri	10	Wyoming	1

The Supreme Court decided, on 17 Feb. 1964, that the Federal Constitution requires congressional districts within each state to be substantially equal in population. By almost invariable custom the Representative lives in the district from which he is elected.

Representatives must not be less than 25 years, citizens of the USA for

7 years and residents in the states from which they are chosen. The House also admits a 'resident commissioner' from Puerto Rico, who has the right to speak on any subject and to make motions, but not to vote; he is elected in the same manner as the Representatives but for a 4-year term. Each of the two Houses of Congress is sole 'judge of the elections, returns and qualifications of its own members'; and each of the Houses may, with the concurrence of two-thirds, expel a Member. The period usually termed 'a Congress' in legislative language, continues for 2 years, terminating at noon on 3 Jan.

No Senator or Representative can, during the time for which he is elected, be appointed to any civil office under authority of the USA which shall have been created, or the emoluments of which shall have been increased, during such time; and no person holding any office under the USA can be a member of either House during his continuance in office. No religious test may be required as a qualification to any office or public trust under the USA or in any state.

STATE LEGISLATURES

Many of the legislatures of the individual states are modelled on the Congress of the USA. The Lieutenant-Governor, by virtue of that office, serves as presiding officer in the Senate. The presiding officer of the House is the Speaker, who is elected by the House from among its Members. The Speaker is the leader of the majority party as well as presiding officer. In the Senate the leader of the majority is the President, *pro tempore,* who presides in the absence of the Lieutenant-Governor.

The general pattern of how legislation is enacted is that a citizen, or legislator, has a suggestion for legislation. The legislator has a Bill prepared outlining the problem and how to deal with it. The Bill is filed, numbered and assigned to committee for study. Introduction constitutes first reading of a Bill, which then must pass every step outlined below. If it fails at any point, the Bill is eliminated from further consideration. Much of the work of a legislature is done by specialised committees. The committee studies the Bill and invites interested persons to give their opinions, and later the committee votes on the Bill. If the committee votes to change or to pass a Bill, the committee reports its recommendations to the House. The Bill is considered by the entire House. Amendments may be presented by any legislator and voted upon. If the Bill passes, it advances to third reading. Final consideration and debate on a Bill occur on third reading. If it passes, the Bill goes to the other House. After it passes the first House, a Bill is sent to the second House where it goes through the same basic steps.

A Bill must pass both Houses in exactly the same form. If there are differences, a Conference Committee from both Houses is generally appointed.

Every Bill is presented to the Governor. If he signs a Bill or files it without signature, it becomes law. If he vetoes it, a Bill is returned to the legislature for reconsideration. Vetoed Bills must be voted upon again by the General Assembly. Because a vetoed Bill has already passed every stage in the process, only a final vote is required. If both Houses reapprove a vetoed Bill, it becomes law despite the veto.

Alabama

The legislature is bicameral and consists of a Senate of 35 Members and a House of Representatives of 106 Members, all elected for a 4-year term. The Governor and Lieutenant-Governor are elected for a 4-year term. Applicants for registration must take an 'anti-communist oath' and fill out a questionnaire to the satisfaction of the registrars. In 10 of the 67 counties, Negroes constitute 50 per cent or more of the population. The State is represented in Congress by 2 Senators and 7 Representatives.

Alaska

The legislature is bicameral and consists of a Senate of 20 Members elected for a 4-year term, and a House of Representatives of 40 Members elected for a 2-year term. The franchise may be exercised by all citizens over 18 years. A Member of the legislature must be a qualified voter and have been resident in Alaska for 3 years. A Senator must be 25 years and a Representative 21 years. The State sends 2 Senators and 1 Representative to Congress.

Arizona

The Senate is bicameral and consists of 30 Members and the House of Representatives of 60, all elected for a 2-year term. Arizona sends to Congress 2 Senators and 4 Representatives.

Arkansas

The General Assembly is bicameral and consists of a Senate of 35 Members, elected for a 4-year term, partially renewed every 2 years, and a House of Representatives of 100 Members elected for a 2-year term. The Sessions are biennial and usually limited to 60 days. The Governor and Lieutenant-Governor are elected for a 2-year term. The State is represented in Congress by 2 Senators and 4 Representatives.

California

The Senate is bicameral and composed of 40 Members elected for a 4-year term, half being elected every 2 years, and the Assembly, of 80 Members, elected for a 2-year term. The Governor and the Lieutenant-Governor are elected for a 4-year term. California is represented in Congress by 2 Senators and 43 Representatives.

Colorado

The General Assembly is bicameral consisting of a Senate of 35 Members elected for a 4-year term, one-half retiring every 2 years, and a House of Representatives of 65 Members elected for a 2-year term. The Governor, Lieutenant-Governor, Attorney-General and Secretary of State are elected for a 4-year term. Qualified as electors are all citizens, male and female (except criminals and insane), over 18 years who have resided in the State for 12 months immediately preceding the election. The State sends to Congress 2 Senators and 5 Representatives.

Connecticut

The General Assembly is bicameral and consists of a Senate of 36 Members and a House of Representatives of 177 Members. Members of each House are elected for a 2-year term. Legislative sessions are annual. The Governor and Lieutenant-Governor are elected for a 4-year term. All citizens (with necessary exceptions and the usual residential requirements) have the right of suffrage. The State is represented in Congress by 2 Senators and 6 Representatives.

Delaware

The General Assembly is bicameral and consists of a Senate of 19 Members elected for a 4-year term, and a House of Representatives of 39 Members elected for a 2-year term. The Governor and Lieutenant-Governor are elected for a 4-year term. With necessary exceptions, all adult citizens, registered as voters, who have resided in the State 1 year and complied with local residential requirements, have the right to vote; those who have attained the age of 18 since 1900 must be able to read English and to write their names. Delaware is represented in Congress by 2 Senators and 1 Representative, elected by the voters of the whole State.

District of Columbia

A reorganisation plan of 1967, submitted by the President to Congress on 1 June 1967, abolished the Commission form of government and instituted a new Mayor-Council form of government. The Mayor, with the title of Commissioner, is appointed by the President, with the advice and consent of the Senate, and is appointed for a 4-year term. The 9-member city council is also appointed by the President. They are appointed with a view to achieving community representation. Congress alone enacts legislation and appropriates m ɔney for municipal expenses. A proposal to grant local self-government was discussed by Congress in 1950 and 1951, and legislation to that end was passed by the House and Senate, but no law has been enacted. The 23rd amendment to the Federal Constitution (1961) conferred the right to vote in national elections.

Florida

The legislature is bicameral consisting of a Senate of 40 Members, elected for a 4-year term, and a House of Representatives with 120 Members elected for a 2-year term. Sessions are held annually, and are limited to 60 days. The Governor is elected for a 4-year term. Two Senators and 15 Representatives are elected to Congress.

Georgia

The General Assembly is bicameral and consists of a Senate of 56 Members and a House of Representatives of 180 Members, both elected for a 2-year term. The Governor and Lieutenant-Governor are elected for a 4-year term. Georgia was the first state to extend the franchise to all citizens of 18 years and above. The State is represented in Congress by 2 Senators and 10 Representatives.

Hawaii

The legislature is bicameral, consisting of a Senate of 25 Members elected for a 4-year term, and a House of Representatives of 51 Members elected for a 2-year term. The Constitution provides for annual meetings of the legislature with 60-day regular sessions. The Governor and Lieutenant-Governor are elected for a 4-year term. The State sends to Congress 2 Senators and 2 Representatives.

Idaho

The legislature is bicameral and consists of a Senate of 35 Members and a House of Representatives of 70 Members, all the legislators being elected for a 2-year term. Annual sessions last for 60 days and 30 days for extraordinary sessions. The Governor, Lieutenant-Governor and Secretary of State are elected for a 4-year term. Voters are citizens over 18 years, who have resided in the State for over 6 months. The State is represented in Congress by 2 Senators and 2 Representatives.

Illinois

The General Assembly is bicameral, consisting of a House of Representatives of 177 Members, elected for a 2-year term, and a Senate of 59 Members who serve 2 terms of 4 years and 1 of 2 years, during a decade. Sessions are annual. The Governor, Lieutenant-Governor and Secretary of State are elected for a 4-year term. Electors are citizens over 18 years having the usual residential qualifications. The State is divided into legislative districts, in each of which 1 Senator and 3 Representatives are chosen; for the election of the latter each elector has 3 votes, of which he may cast 3 for 1 candidate or distribute them equally among no more than 3 candidates. The legislative pattern of Illinois is similar to that of the Congress of USA. The Constitution provides that every Bill shall be read 3 different days in each House, that the Bill and all amendments shall be printed before a vote is taken, and that every Bill, having passed both Houses, shall be signed by the respective Speakers. Bills become law on 1 July at the end of the fiscal year in which passed, except when an emergency exists when by two-thirds majority in both Houses a Bill may become law at once. The Governor may veto a Bill, or parts of a Bill, sent to him. It is then returned to the House in which it originated. The veto may be overridden by two-thirds of Members elected. A Bill may also become law if the Governor fails to return it within 10 days after it has been presented to him, unless the General Assembly, by adjournment, prevents its return. In such case the Bill must be filed within 10 days in the office of the Secretary of State, with the Governor's objections, or it becomes a law. Illinois is represented in Congress by 2 Senators and 24 Representatives.

Indiana

The General Assembly is bicameral, consisting of a Senate of 50 Members elected for a 4-year term, and a House of Representatives of 100 Members elected for a 2-year term. The Governor and Lieutenant-Governor are elected for a 4-year term. The State is represented in Congress by 2 Senators and 11 Representatives.

F

Iowa

The General Assembly is bicameral and comprises a Senate of 50, and a House of Representatives of 100, Members, meeting annually for an unlimited session. Senators are elected for a 4-year term, half retiring every second year; Representatives for a 2-year term. The Governor and Lieutenant-Governor are elected for a 2-year term. The State is represented in Congress by 2 Senators and 6 Representatives.

Kansas

The legislature is bicameral, consisting of a Senate of 40 Members, elected for a 4-year term, and a House of Representatives of 125 Members, elected for a 2-year term. The Governor and Lieutenant-Governor are elected for a 2-year term. The right to vote is (with the usual exceptions) possessed by all citizens. The State was the first of 42 states to establish, in 1933, a Legislative Council of 10 Senators and 15 Representatives, to sit continuously between sessions for the study of legislative problems. The State is represented in Congress by 2 Senators and 5 Representatives.

Kentucky

The General Assembly is bicameral and consists of a Senate of 38 Members elected for a 4-year term, one-half retiring every 2 years, and a House of Representatives of 100 Members elected for a 2-year term. Sessions are biennial. The Governor and Lieutenant-Governor are elected for a 4-year term. All citizens are (with necessary exceptions) qualified as electors; the voting age was, in 1955, reduced from 21 to 18 years. The State is represented in Congress by 2 Senators and 7 Representatives.

Louisiana

The legislature is bicameral and consists of a Senate of 29 Members and a House of Representatives of 105 Members, both chosen for a 4-year term. Sessions are annual; a fiscal session is held in odd years. The Governor and Lieutenant-Governor are elected for a 4-year term. A Governor may serve a second consecutive term. Qualified electors are (with the usual exceptions) all registered citizens with the usual residential qualifications. The State sends to Congress 2 Senators and 8 Representatives.

Maine

The legislature is bicameral and consists of the Senate with 32 Members and the House of Representatives with 151 Members, both Houses being elected simultaneously for a 2-year term. Apart from these legislators and the Governor (elected for a 4-year term), no other state officers are elected. An Executive Council of 7, which meets at the call of the Governor, has effective powers of approval or veto in many matters. The Justices of the Supreme Judicial Court give their opinion upon important questions of law and upon solemn occasions when required by the Governor, Council, Senate, or House of Representatives. The suffrage is possessed by all citizens over 20 years; persons under guardianship for reasons of mental illness have no vote. Indians residing on tribal reservations and otherwise qualified have the vote in all county, state and national elections, but retain the right to elect their own tribal representative to the legislature. The State sends to Congress 2 Senators and 2 Representatives.

Maryland

The General Assembly is bicameral, consisting of a Senate of 43 Members, and a House of Delegates of 142 Members, both elected for a 4-year term. Voters are citizens who have the usual residential qualifications. Maryland sends to Congress 2 Senators and 8 Representatives.

Massachusetts

The legislative body, styled the General Court of the Commonwealth of Massachusetts, is bicameral, meets annually, and consists of the Senate with 40 Members, elected biennially, and the House of Representatives of 240 Members, elected for a 2-year term in 175 districts, each of which returns 1, 2 or 3 Representatives according to the number of legal voters. The Governor and Lieutenant-Governor are elected for a 4-year term. The State sends 2 Senators and 12 Representatives to Congress. Electors are all citizens over 18 years with a 6-months' residence in the Commonwealth.

Michigan

The Senate consists of 38 Members, elected for a 4-year term, and the House of Representatives of 110 Members, elected for a 2-year term. These two Houses make up the bicameral legislature of Michigan. The Governor and Lieutenant-Governor are elected for a 4-year term. Electors are all citizens over 18 years meeting the usual residential requirements. The State sends to Congress 2 Senators and 19 Representatives.

Minnesota

The legislature is bicameral, consisting of a Senate of 67 Members, elected for a 4-year term, and a House of Representatives of 134 Members, elected for a 2-year term. The Governor and Lieutenant-Governor are elected for a 4-year term. The State sends to Congress 2 Senators and 8 Representatives.

Mississippi

The legislature is bicameral, consisting of a Senate of 52 Members and a House of Representatives of 122 Members, both elected for a 4-year term, as are also the Governor and Lieutenant-Governor. The State is represented in Congress by 2 Senators and 5 Representatives.

Missouri

The General Assembly is bicameral, consisting of a Senate of 34 Members elected for a 4-year term (half for re-election every 2 years), and a House of Representatives of 163 Members elected for a 2-year term. The Governor and Lieutenant-Governor are elected for a 4-year term. Voters, with the usual exceptions, are all citizens and those adult aliens who, within a prescribed period, have applied for citizenship. No record is kept of the qualified voters. Missouri sends to Congress 2 Senators and 10 Representatives.

Montana

A new Constitution was adopted on 20 June 1972, and was fully implemented by 1 July 1973; the Senate consists of 40–50 Senators, elected for a 4-year term, one half at each biennial election. The 80–100 Members of the House of Representatives are elected for a 2-year term; these two Houses make up the bicameral legislature of Montana. Electors must be US citizens and resident in the State and over 18 years. The Governor and Lieutenant-Governor are elected for 4-year terms. Montana sends to Congress 2 Senators and 2 Representatives.

Nebraska

By an amendment adopted in Nov. 1934, Nebraska has a unicameral legislature, elected for a 4-year term, of 49 Members. The Governor and Lieutenant-Governor are elected for a 4-year term. Amendments adopted in 1912 and 1920 provide for legislation through the initiative and referendum, and permit cities of more than 5,000 inhabitants to frame their own charters. Nebraska is represented in Congress by 2 Senators and 3 Representatives.

Nevada

The legislature is bicameral, meets biennially and in special sessions, and consists of a Senate of 20 Members elected for a 4-year term, half their number retiring every 2 years, and an Assembly of 40 Members elected for a 2-year term. The Governor, Lieutenant-Governor and Attorney-General are elected for a 4-year term. Qualified electors are all citizens with the usual residential qualifications. Nevada is represented in Congress by 2 Senators and 1 Representative.

New Hampshire

The legislature is bicameral, consisting of a Senate of 30 Members, elected for a 2-year term, and a House of Representatives, restricted to between 375 and 400 Members, elected for a 2-year term. The Governor and 5 administrative officers called 'Councillors' are also elected for a 2-year term. Electors must be adult citizens, able to read and write, duly registered and not paupers or under sentence for crime. New Hampshire sends to the Federal Congress 2 Senators and 2 Representatives.

New Jersey

The legislative power is bicameral and is vested in a Senate and a General Assembly, the members of which are chosen by the people, all citizens (with necessary exceptions) over 18 years, with the usual residential qualifications, having the right of suffrage. The present Constitution, ratified by the voters on 4 Nov. 1947, has been amended 12 times. The Constitutional Convention proposed, and the people adopted in 1966, a new plan providing for a 40-member Senate and an 80-member General Assembly. This plan, as modified by the courts and implemented by the Apportionment Commission, provides for 15 Senate districts, each composed of 1, 2 or 3 whole counties, among which the 40 Senators are apportioned on the basis of population. The Senators are elected from these Senate districts, except that in the multi-member Senate districts composed of more than one county, they are elected one from each sub-district (Assembly district). The State sends to Congress 2 Senators and 15 Representatives.

New Mexico

The state legislature is bicameral and meets annually, consisting of 42 Members of the Senate, elected for a 4-year term, and 70 Members of the House of Representatives, elected for a 2-year term. The Governor and Lieutenant-Governor are elected for a 4-year term. The State sends to Congress 2 Senators and 2 Representatives.

New York

The Constitutional Convention of 1967 (4 Apr. to 26 Sept.) was composed of 186 Delegates who proposed a new State Constitution; however, this was rejected by the registered voters on 7 Nov. 1967. The Senate consists of 57 Members, and the Assembly of 150 Members, both elected for a 2-year term. These two Houses make up the bicameral legislature of New York State. The Governor and Lieutenant-Governor are elected for a 4-year term. The right of suffrage resides in every adult who has been a citizen for 90 days, and has the usual residential qualifications; new voters must establish, by certificates or test, that they have had at least an elementary education. The State is represented in Congress by 2 Senators and 39 Representatives.

North Carolina

The General Assembly is bicameral and consists of a Senate of 50 Members and a House of Representatives of 120 Members, elected for a 2-year term. The Governor and Lieutenant-Governor are elected for a 4-year term. The Governor may not succeed himself, and has no veto. All registered citizens with the usual residential qualifications have a vote. The State is represented in Congress by 2 Senators and 11 Representatives.

North Dakota

The Legislative Assembly is bicameral and consists of a Senate of 51 Members elected for a 4-year term, and a House of Representatives of

102 Members elected for a 2-year term. The Governor and Lieutenant-Governor are elected for a 4-year term. Qualified electors are (with necessary exceptions) all citizens and civilised Indians. Bills may be initiated in either House, but may not be initiated by the Governor, although he may recommend measures to the Assembly and is responsible for the execution of all laws which the Assembly has passed. He has a veto on legislation, which may be overridden if the measure is passed again by a majority of both Houses. The State sends to Congress 2 Senators elected by the voters of the entire State, and 1 Representative.

Ohio

The General Assembly is bicameral and the Senate consists of 33 Members and the House of Representatives of 99 Members. The Senate is elected for a 4-year term, half each 2 years; the House is elected for a 2-year term; the Governor, Lieutenant-Governor and Secretary of State for a 4-year term. Qualified electors are (with necessary exceptions) all citizens over 18 years who have the usual residential qualifications. Ohio sends 2 Senators and 23 Representatives to Congress.

Oklahoma

The legislature is bicameral, consisting of a Senate of 48 Members, who are elected for a 4-year term, and a House of Representatives consisting of 101 Members, elected for a 2-year term. The Governor and Lieutenant-Governor are elected for a 4-year term; the Governor can only be elected for two terms in succession. Electors are (with necessary exceptions) all citizens over 18 years with the usual qualifications. Indians are qualified as voters. The State is represented in Congress by 2 Senators and 6 Representatives.

Oregon

The Legislative Assembly is bicameral and consists of a Senate of 30 Members, elected for a 4-year term, half their number retiring every 2 years, and a House of 60 Representatives, elected for a 2-year term. The Governor is elected for a 4-year term. The Constitution reserves to the voters the rights of initiative and referendum, and recall. The State sends to Congress 2 Senators and 4 Representatives.

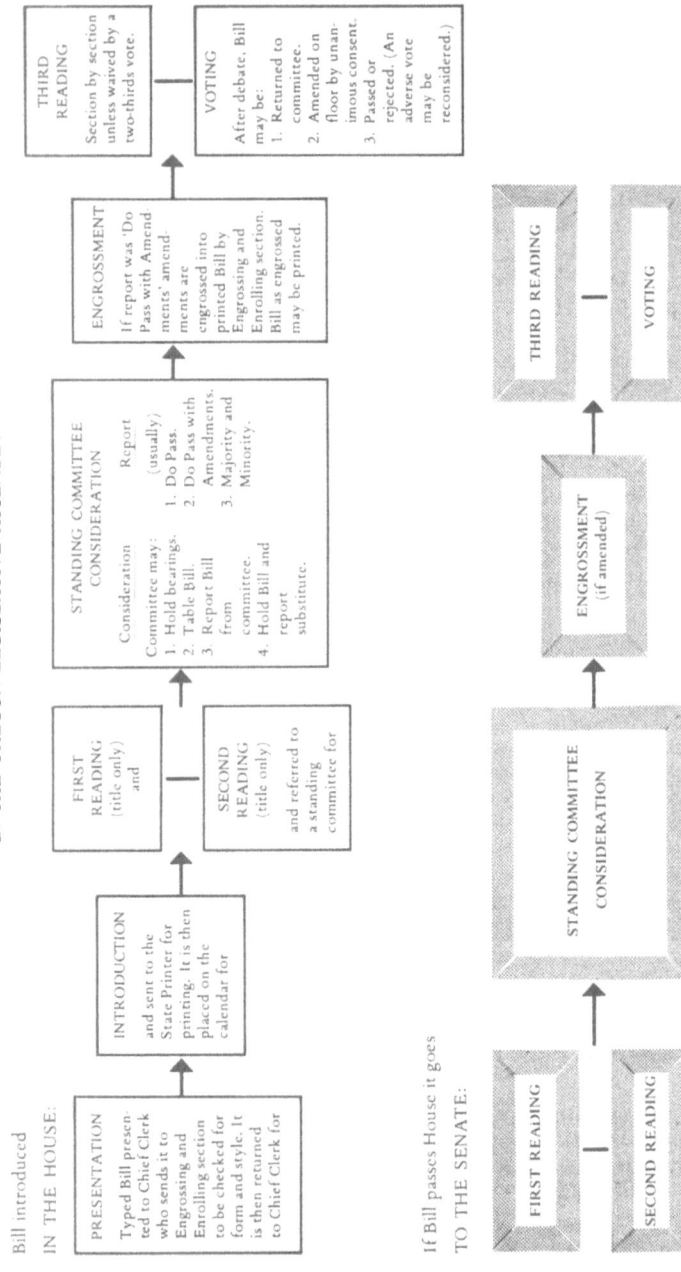

STEPS IN ENACTING A HOUSE BILL
IN THE OREGON LEGISLATIVE ASSEMBLY

Bill introduced
IN THE HOUSE:

PRESENTATION
Typed Bill presented to Chief Clerk who sends it to Engrossing and Enrolling section to be checked for form and style. It is then returned to Chief Clerk for

INTRODUCTION
and sent to the State Printer for printing. It is then placed on the calendar for

FIRST READING (title only) and

SECOND READING (title only) and referred to a standing committee for

STANDING COMMITTEE CONSIDERATION

Consideration

Committee may:
1. Hold hearings.
2. Table Bill
3. Report Bill from committee.
4. Hold Bill and report substitute.

Report (usually)
1. Do Pass.
2. Do Pass with Amendments.
3. Majority and Minority.

ENGROSSMENT
If report was 'Do Pass with Amendments amendments are engrossed into printed Bill by Engrossing and Enrolling section. Bill as engrossed may be printed.

THIRD READING
Section by section unless waived by a two-thirds vote.

VOTING
After debate, Bill may be:
1. Returned to committee.
2. Amended on floor by unanimous consent.
3. Passed or rejected. (An adverse vote may be reconsidered.)

If Bill passes House it goes
TO THE SENATE:

FIRST READING

SECOND READING

STANDING COMMITTEE CONSIDERATION

ENGROSSMENT (if amended)

THIRD READING

VOTING

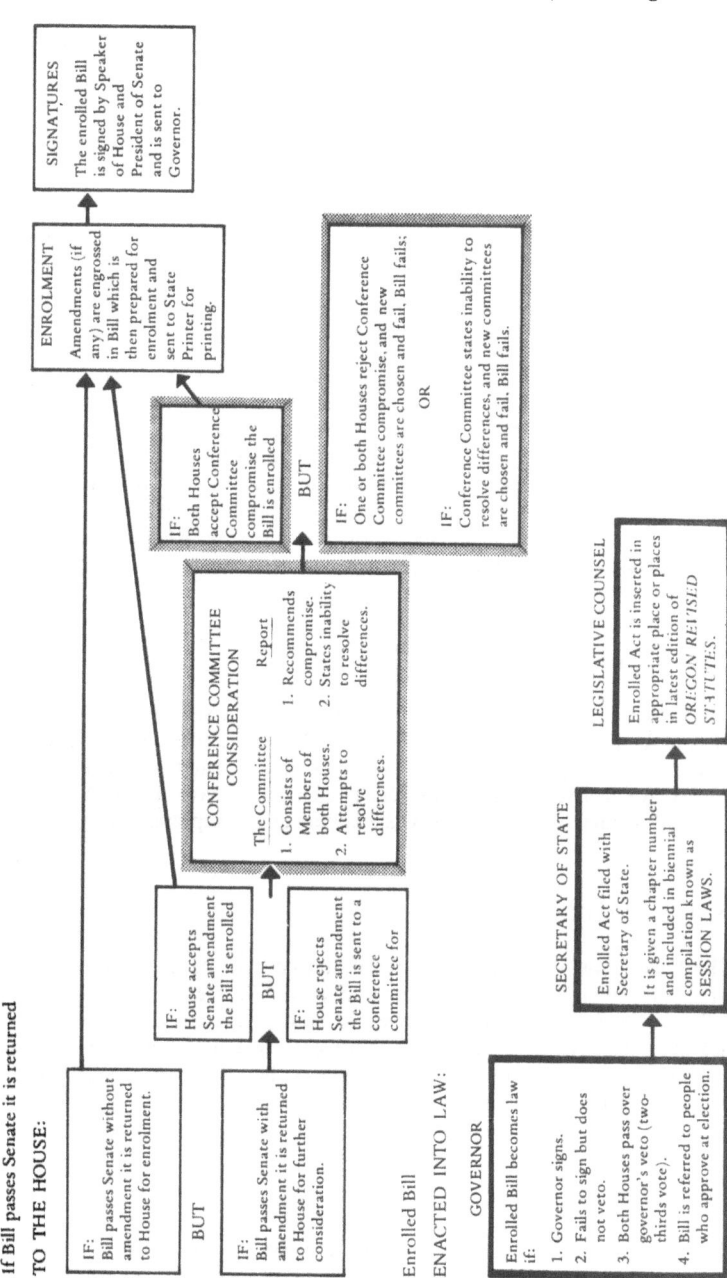

If Bill passes Senate it is returned

TO THE HOUSE:

IF:
Bill passes Senate without amendment it is returned to House for enrolment.

BUT

IF:
Bill passes Senate with amendment it is returned to House for further consideration.

IF:
House accepts Senate amendment the Bill is enrolled

BUT

IF:
House rejects Senate amendment the Bill is sent to a conference committee for

CONFERENCE COMMITTEE CONSIDERATION

The Committee
1. Consists of Members of both Houses.
2. Attempts to resolve differences.

Report
1. Recommends compromise.
2. States inability to resolve differences.

IF:
Both Houses accept Conference Committee compromise the Bill is enrolled

BUT

IF:
One or both Houses reject Conference Committee compromise, and new committees are chosen and fail, Bill fails.

OR

IF:
Conference Committee states inability to resolve differences, and new committees are chosen and fail. Bill fails.

ENROLMENT
Amendments (if any) are engrossed in Bill which is then prepared for enrolment and sent to State Printer for printing.

SIGNATURES
The enrolled Bill is signed by Speaker of House and President of Senate and is sent to Governor.

Enrolled Bill

ENACTED INTO LAW:

GOVERNOR

Enrolled Bill becomes law if:
1. Governor signs.
2. Fails to sign but does not veto.
3. Both Houses pass over governor's veto (two-thirds vote).
4. Bill is referred to people who approve at election.

SECRETARY OF STATE

Enrolled Act filed with Secretary of State.

It is given a chapter number and included in biennial compilation known as SESSION LAWS.

LEGISLATIVE COUNSEL

Enrolled Act is inserted in appropriate place or places in latest edition of *OREGON REVISED STATUTES*.

Pennsylvania

The General Assembly is bicameral and consists of a Senate of 50 Members chosen for a 4-year term, one-half being elected biennially, and a House of Representatives of 203 Members chosen for a 2-year term. The Governor and Lieutenant-Governor are elected for a 4-year term. Every citizen over 18 years, with the usual residential qualifications, may vote. The State sends to Congress 2 Senators and 25 Representatives.

Rhode Island

The General Assembly is bicameral, consisting of a Senate of 50 Members and a House of Representatives of 100 Members, both elected for a 2-year term, as are also the Governor and Lieutenant-Governor. Rhode Island's Constitution of 1842, which finally replaced the King Charles Charter 66 years after the Declaration of Independence, vested legislative power in the General Assembly. Every citizen over 18 years who has resided in the State for 30 days and is duly registered, is qualified to vote. Rhode Island sends to Congress 2 Senators and 2 Representatives.

South Carolina

The General Assembly is bicameral and consists of a Senate of 46 Members, elected for a 4-year term, and a House of Representatives of 124 Members, elected for a 2-year term. The Governor and Lieutenant-Governor are elected for a 4-year term. Only registered citizens have the right to vote. South Carolina sends to Congress 2 Senators and 6 Representatives.

South Dakota

The Legislative Assembly is bicameral and consists of the Senate with 35 Members, and the House of Representatives with 75 Members, all elected for a 2-year term, as are also the Governor and Lieutenant-Governor. Voters are all citizens over 18 years who have complied with certain residential qualifications. The people reserve the right of the initiative and referendum. The State sends 2 Senators and 2 Representatives to Congress.

Tennessee

The General Assembly is bicameral and consists of a Senate of 33 Members and a House of Representatives of 99 Members. Senators are elected for a

4-year term and Representatives for a 2-year term. No clergyman of any denomination is eligible to either House. Electors must be citizens, with the usual residential qualifications and over 18 years. Tennessee sends to Congress 2 Senators and 8 Representatives.

Texas

The legislature is bicameral and consists of a Senate of 31 Members elected for a 4-year term, half their number retiring every 2 years, and a House of Representatives of 150 Members elected for a 2-year term. The Governor and Lieutenant-Governor are elected for a 2-year term. Electors are all citizens with the usual residential qualifications. Texas sends to Congress 2 Senators and 24 Representatives.

Utah

The legislature is bicameral and consists of a Senate (in part renewed every 2 years) of 30 Members, elected for a 4-year term, and of a House of Representatives of 69 Members elected for a 2-year term. The Governor is elected for a 4-year term. The Constitution provides for the initiative and referendum. Electors are all citizens, who, not being insane or criminal, have the usual residential qualifications. The State sends to Congress 2 Senators and 2 Representatives.

Vermont

In 1793 a Constitution was adopted which, with amendments, is still in force. The state legislature is bicameral, consisting of a Senate of 30 Members and a House of Representatives of 150 Members, both elected for a 2-year term. The Governor and Lieutenant-Governor are elected for a 2-year term. Electors are all citizens who possess certain residential qualifications and have taken the freeman's oath set forth in the Constitution. The State sends to Congress 2 Senators and 1 Representative, who are elected by the voters of the entire State.

Virginia

The General Assembly is bicameral and consists of a Senate of 40 Members, elected for a 4-year term, and a House of Delegates of 100 Members, elected for a 2-year term. The Governor and Lieutenant-Governor are elected for a 4-year term. Electors are, with few exceptions, all citizens over 21 years fulfilling certain residential qualifications, who have registered. The State sends to Congress 2 Senators and 10 Representatives.

Washington

The legislature is bicameral, consisting of a Senate of 49 Members elected for a 4-year term, half their number retiring every 2 years, and a House of Representatives of 98 Members elected for a 2-year term. The Governor and Lieutenant-Governor are elected for a 4-year term. Electors are, with some exceptions, all citizens over 18 years having the usual residential qualifications. The State sends 2 Senators and 7 Representatives to Congress.

West Virginia

The legislature is bicameral and consists of the Senate of 34 Members elected for a 4-year term, one-half being elected biennially, and the House of Delegates of 100 Members, elected biennially. The Governor is elected for a 4-year term. Voters are all citizens, with the usual exceptions, over 18 years, who meet certain residential requirements. The State sends to Congress 2 Senators and 4 Representatives.

Wisconsin

The legislative power is bicameral and vested in a Senate of 33 Members (1971 term: 13 Democrats and 20 Republicans), elected for a 4-year term, one-half elected alternately, and an Assembly of 99 Members (1971 term [100 Members]: 66 Democrats and 18 Republicans), all elected simultaneously for a 2-year term. The Governor and Lieutenant-Governor are elected for a 4-year term. There is universal suffrage for all citizens over 18 years but, as there is no official list of voters, the size of the electorate is unknown. Wisconsin is represented in Congress by 2 Senators and 9 Representatives.

Wyoming

The legislature is bicameral and consists of a Senate of 30 Members elected for a 4-year term, and a House of Representatives of 61 Members elected for a 2-year term. The Governor is elected for a 4-year term. The suffrage extends to all citizens, male and female, who can read, and who have the usual residential qualifications. The State sends to Congress 2 Senators and 1 Representative, elected by the voters of the entire State.

OUTLYING TERRITORIES

Guam

The legislature is unicameral and the powers are similar to those of an American state legislature. All adults over 18 years are enfranchised.

Puerto Rico

Citizens of Puerto Rico do not vote in the US presidential elections, though individuals living on the mainland are free to do so subject to the local electoral laws. The legislature is bicameral. The Senate is composed of 27 Members and the House of Representatives, 51 Members. All citizens over 21 years may vote. Puerto Rico sends to Congress a Resident Commissioner to the US, elected by the people for a 4-year term. But he has no vote in Congress, and under the doctrine of 'no taxation without representation' Puerto Rico is not subject to US taxes. Males, however, are subject to conscription. In 1953 President Eisenhower sent a message to the General Assembly of the UN stating 'if at any time the Legislative Assembly of Puerto Rico adopts a resolution in favour of more complete or even absolute independence' he 'will immediately thereafter recommend to Congress that such independence be granted'. The new Constitution was drafted by a Puerto Rican Constituent Assembly and approved by the electorate at a referendum in 1952. It was then submitted to Congress, which struck out Section 20 of Article 11 covering the 'right to work' and the 'right to an adequate standard of living'; the remainder was passed and proclaimed by the Governor.

American Samoa

On 25 Feb. 1948 a bicameral legislature was established, at the request of the Samoans, to have advisory legislative functions. With the adoption of the Revised Constitution of American Samoa in 1967, the legislature was vested with limited law-making authority. The Lower House, or House of Representatives, is composed of 20 Members elected by universal adult suffrage. The Upper House, or Senate, is composed of 18 Members elected, in the traditional Samoan manner, in meetings of the Chiefs.

Trust Territory of the Pacific Islands

Legislative authority, previously exercised by the High Commissioner, was officially transferred in 1965 to the 33-member bicameral Congress of Micronesia. There are 12 Senators, two elected at large from each of the six administrative districts, for a 4-year term. The House of Representatives has 21 Members elected for a 2-year term from single-member representative districts. Members of the Congress of Micronesia are chosen by secret ballots in biennial elections. All citizens of the Trust Territory who are 18 years or over are eligible to vote. There is a regular session of the Congress of Micronesia held each year, beginning on the second Monday in January and continuing for 50 consecutive calendar days. The High Commissioner may call a special session whenever he deems it necessary.

The Virgin Islands

The Organic Act of 22 July 1954 gives the US Department of the Interior full jurisdiction. Some limited legislative powers are given to a unicameral legislature, composed of 15 Senators elected for a 2-year term. The Governor was formerly appointed by the President, with the consent of the Senate, for an indefinite term. In 1970 the islanders elected a Governor for the first time. The franchise is vested in residents who are citizens of the United States, over 21 years. They do not participate in the US presidential election and have no representative in Congress.

UPPER VOLTA

Legislative power was exercised by the National Assembly. The 57 Members were elected for a 5-year term. Elections were by universal adult (at 21 years) suffrage. In Feb. 1974 the Constitution was suspended and the National Assembly dissolved.

URUGUAY

Parliament (*Asamblea General*) was dissolved by Presidential decree in 1973. Previously Parliament had been bicameral, consisting of a Senate (*Senado*) of 31 Members and a Chamber of Representatives (*Cámara de Representantes*) of 99 Members.

VATICAN CITY STATE

The Vatican City State is governed by a Commission appointed by the Pope. The reason for the City State's existence is to provide an extra-territorial, independent base for the Holy See, the Government of the Roman Catholic Church.

VENEZUELA

Congress (*Congreso Nacional*) is bicameral and consists of a Senate (*Senado*) and a Chamber of Deputies (*Cámara de Diputados*). At least 2 Senators are elected for each state and for the federal district. Senators must be Venezuelans by birth, and over 30 years. Deputies must be native Venezuelans over 21 years; there is 1 for every 50,000 inhabitants. The territories, on reaching the population fixed by law, also elect Deputies. Voting, by proportional representation, is compulsory for men and women over 18. Owing to the high rate of illiteracy, voting is by coloured ballot cards. The President must be a Venezuelan by birth and over 30 years; he has a qualified power of veto.

NORTH VIETNAM (DEMOCRATIC REPUBLIC OF VIETNAM)

The National Assembly (*Quoc Hoi*) of 420 Deputies has a 4-year term and meets twice a year. It has a permanent executive body in its Standing Committee. All citizens may vote at 18 and be elected to office at 21. Rural constituencies contain 50,000 electors; urban 10,000–30,000. The President of the Republic is elected by the National Assembly, and the Great Council consists of the Premier, Vice-Premiers and other Ministers.

SOUTH VIETNAM (REPUBLIC OF VIETNAM)

Legislative power is exercised by the National Assembly (*Quoc Hoi*) which is bicameral. A House of Representatives (*Ha-Hghi-Vien*) of 159 Members is elected for a 4-year term and a Senate (*Thuong-Hghi-Vien*) of 30–60 Members is elected for a 6-year term. Adult suffrage is at 18 years. All Members of the House of Representatives must be over 25 years, and of the Senate, 30 years.

WESTERN SAMOA

The Constitution provides for a Head of State known as *Ao o le Malo*, which position from 1 Jan. 1962 was held jointly by the representatives of the two royal lines of Tuiaana/Tuiatua and Malietoa. On the death of HH Tupua Tamasese Mea'ole, CBE, on 5 Apr. 1963, HH Malietoa Tanumafili II, CBE, became, as provided by the Constitution, the sole Head of State for life. Future Heads of State will be elected by the Legislative Assembly and hold office for a 5-year term. Parliament comprises the Head of State and the Legislative Assembly. The Legislative Assembly has 45 Members elected from territorial constituencies on a franchise confined to *matais* or chiefs (of whom there are about 11,000), and 2 Members elected on universal adult suffrage from the individual voters' roll, which has replaced the old European roll.

YEMEN ARAB REPUBLIC

In 1970 a new Constitution was promulgated and elections for a Consultative Council took place in 1971. There were 179 Members of whom 159 were indirectly elected, for a 4-year term, by village council representatives and 20 appointed by the Chairman of the Republican Council. In June 1974 a Military Command Council took power and the Constitution and Consultative Council were suspended 'until the Republic's affairs are restored to their normal course'.

YUGOSLAVIA

The Federal Assembly (*Savezna Skupština*) is the supreme organ of government and social self-government of the Federation. It has 5 Chambers (Federal, Economic, Education and Culture, Social Welfare and Health and Organisational-Political); every Chamber has 120 Deputies. The Federal Chamber comprises 140 Members delegated by the 6 republics (20 from each) and 2 autonomous provinces (10 from each); they sit as a Chamber of Nationalities to safeguard the rights and equality of peoples and republics. The Members of all assemblies are elected for a 4-year term. No person can be elected twice successively as a Member of the same Chamber, or of the Federal Executive Council. The President of the Republic can be re-elected for a second 5-year term. Federal and Republic officials cannot hold the same post longer than 4 years, except when the Assembly approves it. The Federal Assembly, at a joint meeting of all Chambers, elects the President of the Republic, and the President and 6 Vice-Presidents of the Federal Assembly. The functions of the President of the Republic are separated from those of the President of the Federal Executive Council. The President and the Members of the Federal Executive Council are elected by the Federal Chamber from among its Deputies. The Federal Executive Council is the political executive organ of the Federal Assembly. It comprises a Chariman, 2 Vice-Chairmen and 20 Members.

ZAÏRE

The National Assembly (*Assemblée Nationale*) has 420 Members elected for a 5-year term from the single list of the ruling People's Revolutionary Movement (*Mouvement Populaire de la Revolution*).

ZAMBIA

The National Assembly is unicameral and has 136 Members. The increase in membership occurred in 1973 when Zambia became a one-party state. Members are elected for a 5-year term. A Bill must receive Presidential assent before becoming law. If the President returns a Bill it shall not be represented within 6 months, unless two-thirds of Members give it support. Should this occur, the President will give his assent within 3 weeks, or dissolve Parliament.

EUROPEAN ECONOMIC COMMUNITY

The European Parliament, referred to in the Treaties as the Assembly, consists of 198 Members nominated by the 9 national Parliaments: 36 Members for France, West Germany, Italy and UK*, 14 for Belguim and the Netherlands, 10 for Denmark and the Irish Republic and 6 for Luxembourg. The Treaties, however, provide for the eventual direct election of the Parliament's Members by universal suffrage; a draft Convention on the procedure for such elections was passed by the Parliament in 1960 but has not been acted upon by the Council. The Parliament is at present working on new proposals which will take account of the Community's enlargement in 1973.

Under the Treaties, the Council of Ministers is obliged to consult the Parliament on a wide range of legislàtive matters. Under its own rules, the Parliament is also able to hold debates on whatever subjects it chooses, whether these are covered by the Treaties or not. The Parliament's 12 Standing Committees, Political, Legal, Economic and Monetary, Budgets, Social and Employment, Agriculture, Regional and Transport, Public Health and Environment, Energy and Technology, Cultural Affairs and Youth, External Economic Relations, and Development and Cooperation, work closely with the Commission in scrutinising and amending Community legislation. The Parliament has formal power to elicit information on policy from the Commission by written or oral questions, and has also acquired the informal power to question the Council of Ministers. The Parliament can dismiss the Commission on a motion of censure approved by a two-thirds majority, but as yet has no powers of appointment.

At present, the Parliament exercises full budgetary control only over non-mandatory expenditure: *i.e.* expenditure not arising directly from the Treaties. Effectively this means control only over the administrative budget, about 3–4 per cent of the total. However, new powers over the whole Community budget, including the power to reject it in its entirety, are likely to be exercised by the Parliament from 1975. If the Community itself develops into the 'ever closer union of the peoples of Europe' that its founders envisaged, then greater powers for the Parliament, and its direct election, will be essential.

The Members of the Parliament sit, not in national delegations, but in party groups, which together control the Parliament's business: arrangements for debates, appointment of *rapporteurs* to investigate Community legislation, etc. There are at present 6 groups: Communist, Socialist, Christian Democrat, Conservative, European Progressive Democrat, and Liberal. Several Members also sit as Independents.

* The UK has been allocated 36 seats, but the UK Parliamentary Labour Party has decided not to occupy any seats until the renegotiation of UK membership has been completed. The UK delegation has a membership of 21 with 15 vacant seats.

Selected bibliography

GENERAL

The Political Handbook of the World. Annual. New York

Ameller, M., *Parliaments.* London, 1966

Bryce, J., *The American Commonwealth.* 3 vols. 1888

Butler, D. E. (ed.), *Elections Abroad.* London, 1959

Campion, Lord, and Lidderdale, D. W. S., *European Parliamentary Procedure.* London, 1953

— — *Parliaments.* London, 1962

Ehrmann, H. W. (ed.), *Interest Groups in Four Continents.* Univ. of Pittsburgh, 1958

Lakeman, E. and Lambert, J. D., *Voting in Democracies.* London, 1955

Lowell, A. L., *Governments and Parties in Continental Europe.* 2 vols. 1896

Mackenzie, W. J. M., *Free Elections.* London, 1958

Mill, J. S., *Representative Government.* 1861

Ross, J. F. S., *Elections and Electors.* London, 1955

—, *Parliamentary Representation.* London, 1956

Smith, T. E., *Elections in Developing Countries.* London, 1966

Wheare, K. C., *Legislatures.* OUP, 1963

Wilson, W., *Congressional Government.* 1855

EUROPE

Andrén, N., *Government and Politics in the Nordic Countries.* Stockholm, 1964

Arneson, B. A., *The Democratic Monarchies of Scandinavia.* 2nd edition. New York, 1949

Bagehot, W., *The English Constitution.* 1867

Bihari, O., *Socialist Representative Institutions.* Budapest, 1970

Breuer, R., *Nordrhein–Westfalen: Handbuch zur Staatspolitischen Landeskunde der Gegenwart.* Munich, 1967

Bromhead, P. A., *Private Members Bills in the British Parliament.* London, 1956

— *The House of Lords and Contemporary Politics.* London, 1958

Butler, D. E., and Kavanagh, D., *The British General Election of February 1974.* London, 1974.

Butler, D. E., and Pinto-Duschinsky, M., *The British General Election of 1970.* London, 1971

Campbell, P., *French Electoral Systems and Elections, 1789–1957.* London, 1958

Chester, D. N., and Bowring, N., *Questions in Parliament.* Oxford, 1962

Erskine May, T., *The Law, Privileges, Proceedings and Usage of Parliament.* 18th edition. London, 1971

Glum, F., *Die staatsrechtliche Strukturder Bundesrepublik Deutschland: Bund und Länder—Parlament und Regierung.* Bonn, 1965

Gordon, S., *Our Parliament.* 4th edition. London, 1958

Hastad, E., *The Parliament of Sweden.* Hansard Society, 1957

Hiscocks, R., *Democracy in Western Germany.* OUP, 1957

Hoffman, H., *Handbuch zur staatspolitischen landeskunde der Gegenwart.* Munich, 1966

Hughes, C. J., *The Parliament of Switzerland.* Hansard Society, 1962

Ilbert, C., and Carr, C., *Parliament*. 3rd edition. OUP, 1948

Jennings, I., *Parliament*. 3rd edition. OUP, 1960

Kastari, P., *La présidence de la république en Finlande*. Neuchâtel, 1962

King-Hall, S., and Ullman, R. K., *German Parliaments*. Hansard Society, 1956

Kitzinger, U., *German Electoral Politics*. Oxford, 1960

Lammich, S., *Das sozialistische Parlament Polens*. Köln, 1971

Laski, H. J., *Parliamentary Government in England*. London, 1938

Lidderdale, D. W. S., *The Parliament of France*. London, 1951

Lowell, A. L., *The Government of England*. 2 vols. 1908

McCallum, R. B., and Readman, A., *The British General Election of 1945*. OUP, 1947

Maunz, T., *Deutsches Staatsrecht*. 12th edition. Munich, 1963

Merikoski, V., *Précis du Droit Public de la Finlande*. Helsinki, 1954

Morrison, H., *Government and Parliament*. 2nd edition. OUP, 1959

Nicholas, H. G., *The British General Election of 1950*. London, 1951

Nicolson, N., *People and Parliament*. London, 1958

Raalte, E. Van., *The Parliament of the Kingdom of the Netherlands*. Hansard Society, 1959

Redlich, J., *The Procedure of the House of Commons*. 3 vols. 1907

Richards, P. G., *Honourable Members*. London, 1959

Rustow, D. A., *The Politics of Compromise*. Princeton University Press, 1955

Sharp, W. R., *The Government of the French Republic*. New York, 1939

Sipponen, K., *Some Aspects of the Delegation of Legislative Power in Finland*. Scandinavian Studies in Law, 1965

Stewart, J. D., *British Pressure Groups*. Oxford, 1958

Storbeck, A. C., *Die regierungen des bundes und der länder seit 1945*. Munich, 1970

Taylor, E., *The House of Commons at Work*. 3rd edition. London, 1958

Toivola, U. (ed.), *Introduction to Finland 1960*. Helsinki, 1960

— *Constitution Act and Parliament Act of Finland*. Ministry of Foreign Affairs, Helsinki, 1967

Triska, J. F. (ed.), *Constitutions of the Communist Party States*. Stanford, 1968

Williams, P., *Politics in Post-War France*. London, 1954

Williams, W., and Harrison, M., *De Gaulle's Republic*. 2nd edition. London, 1961

Young, R., *The British Parliament*. London, 1962

THE AMERICAS

Quebec Yearbook. Annual

The Book of the States. Two-yearly

The Canada Yearbook. Annual

Beck, M., *The Government of Nova Scotia*. Toronto, 1957

Brady, A., *Democracy in the Dominions*. 2nd edition. University of Toronto Press, 1952

Campbell, G. C., *The History of Nova Scotia*. Toronto, 1968

Dawson, R. McG., *The Government of Canada*. 3rd edition. University of Toronto Press, 1960

Galloway, G. B., *The Legislative Process in Congress*. New York, 1953

Gélinas, A., *Les parliamentaires et l'administration au Québec*. Laval University Press, 1969

Griffith, E. S., *Congress: Its Contemporary Role*. Revised edition. New York, 1956.

Horwood, H., *Newfoundland.* Toronto, 1969

Key, V. O., *Politics, Parties and Pressure Groups.* 4th edition. New York, 1958

MacCourt, E. A., *Saskatchewan.* Toronto, 1968

— *The Yukon and the Northwest Territories.* Toronto, 1969

McInnes, E., *Canada: A Political and Social History.* Revised edition. Toronto, 1959

MacKinnon, F., *The Government of Prince Edward Island.* University of Toronto Press, 1951

Macpherson, C. B., *Democracy in Alberta.* 2nd edition. Toronto, 1962

Mallory, J. R., *The Structure of Canadian Government.* Toronto, 1971

Noel, S. J. R., *Politics in Newfoundland.* University of Toronto Press, 1971

Perlin, A. B., *The Story of Newfoundland, 1497–1959.* St John's, 1959

Riddick, F. M., *The United States Congress: Its Organisation and Procedure.* Manassas, 1949

Robin, M. (ed.), *Canadian Provincial Politics.* Ontario, 1971

Walker, H., *The Legislative Process.* New York, 1948

Wright, J. F. C., *Saskatchewan: The History of a Province.* Toronto, 1955

THE REST OF THE WORLD

New South Wales Parliamentary Record. Edition from 1824. Sydney

Official Yearbook of New South Wales. Annual. Commonwealth Bureau of Census and Statistics, Sydney

Queensland Year Book. Annual. Brisbane

South Australian Year Book. Annual. Commonwealth Bureau of Census and Statistics, Adelaide

Tasmania Year Book. Annual. Commonwealth Bureau of Census and Statistics, Hobart

Bibliography

Victoria: The First Century. Melbourne, 1934

Victorian Yearbook. Annual. Commonwealth Bureau of Census and Statistics, Melbourne

Western Australia Year Book. Annual. Commonwealth Bureau of Census and Statistics, Perth

Baerwald, H. H., *Japan's Parliament.* OUP, 1974

Crisp, L. F., *Parliamentary Government of the Commonwealth of Australia.* London, 1949

Crowley, F. K., and de Garis, B. K., *A Short History of Western Australia.* Melbourne, 1969

Davies, A. F., *Australian Democracy.* London, 1958

Davis, S. R. (ed.), *The Government of the Australian States.* London, 1960

Gibbs, R. M., *A History of South Australia.* Adelaide, 1969

Green, F. C. (ed.), *A Century of Responsible Government.* Hobart, 1956

Hawker, G. N., *The Parliament of New South Wales 1856–1965.* Government Printer, Ultima, 1971

Lack, C., *Three Decades of Queensland Political History.* Brisbane, 1962

Mackenzie, W. J., and Robinson, K. E. (eds.), *Five Elections in Africa.* Oxford, 1960.

Miller, J. D. B., *Australian Government and Politics.* 2nd edition. London, 1959

Morris Jones, W. H., *Parliament in India.* London, 1957

Mukharjea, A. R., *Parliamentary Procedure in India.* OUP, 1958

Sawer, G., *Australian Government Today.* 10th edition. Melbourne University Press, 1970

Wettenhall, R. L., *A Guide to Tasmanian Government Administration.* Hobart, 1968

Glossary

Absolutism   The governed have no representation, vote, or other share in the administration and the ruler of the State has unlimited power.

Anarchism   A political doctrine advocating the abolition of organised authority and that the means of production should be made common. Anarchists hold that all forms of government are oppressive and undesirable, and advocate free associa- tion of individuals, without armed forces, courts, prisons or written law.

Apartheid   Afrikaans word, literally 'apart-hood', meaning racial segrega- tion as practised by the government of the Republic of South Africa since 1948.

Authoritarian   A totalitarian system of government, favouring absolute obedience to authority.

Bicameral   Composed of two legis- lative Chambers. Generally consisting of Upper and Lower Chambers. Both Chambers can usually initiate legisla- tion but the more important and controversial Bills are generally intro- duced in the Lower Chamber.

Centralism   A system under which the state is politically controlled from the capital, as opposed to decentralised systems of administration such as feder- alism and regionalism, under which local units enjoy a greater or lesser degree of autonomy.

165

Congress A formal assembly of representatives to act as a legislature, especially in republics. The bicameral federal legislature of the USA comprises the Senate and the House of Representatives. The US Constitution commences: 'All legislative powers herein granted shall be vested in a Congress of the United States, which shall consist of a Senate and House of Representatives.' Many other countries follow the US Congressional pattern.

Constitution The system of fundamental laws and principles that prescribes the nature, functions and limits of a government.

Constitutional monarchy A monarchy in which the powers of the ruler are restricted to those granted under the Constitution and the Laws of the nation.

Corporate state A system of government in which trade and professional corporations are the basis of society. The corporations represent the employers and the employed in the various branches of the economic life of a country. Parliament is elected not by territorial constituencies but by the corporations.

Coup d'état A sudden change of government brought about by force in violation of constitutional forms. Generally brought about by persons who already hold governmental or military power. It differs from a revolution in that it is effected from above, while a revolution involves the participation of the masses.

Dáil Eireann The Lower House of the Parliament of the Irish Republic.

Democracy Government by the people. Democracy may be either direct, and exerted by popular assemblies or by plebiscites on all legislation, or indirect, and exerted by representative institutions. Direct democracy was practised in some of the city states of ancient Greece; indirect democracy was developed in Britain and by mid-19th century a large proportion of nations had adopted democratic institutions which were better suited to modern states with large populations.

Democracy as accepted in western Europe, the British Commonwealth, and the USA is based on the theory of the separation of power; Legislation being carried out by a freely elected parliament and executive power being vested either in a government responsible to the legislature, as in the UK, or in a President responsible to the people, as in the USA. This implies free choice at regular intervals between two or more parties. An election in which the electorate can only choose or reject a single list of candidates is not democratic in this sense of the word.

Government of the people is interpreted differently in the USSR, and in parts of Asia and eastern Europe. The principles of the separation of powers are not generally accepted but private ownership of the means of production is regarded as undemocratic in these countries.

Dictatorship Absolute or despotic rule of a person or group without the necessity of the consent of the governed.

Federation   A political unit on which a number of smaller political units devolve certain power over themselves and their citizens, and to which they usually entrust the conduct of their foreign affairs. The individual provinces or states, as they are often called, retain some control over their internal affairs, and in order that their rights should be clearly defined there is usually a Federal Constitution which allocates powers between them and the Federal Government.

Initiative   The right of the electorate to instruct Parliament to proceed with a measure. This includes the referendum and recall. In Switzerland, for example, any 50,000 citizens may propose a total or a partial revision of the Federal Constitution.

Lobbying   Influencing legislators to support or oppose a Bill by means of personal contacts, especially in the 'lobbies' or parts of a legislative building to which the public has access. Those sectors of the electorate who attempt to lobby legislators are generally known as pressure groups.

Nationalisation   To convert a sector of industry from private to government control. Nationalisation exists even in countries where private enterprise predominates and has given rise to 'mixed economies'.

Popular Front   The collaboration of Communist, Socialist and other left-wing political parties against reaction and Fascism, originating in Europe in the 1930s.

Proportional Representation   Representation of all parties in a legislature in proportion to their popular vote. This can be calculated in several ways: The simplest being one in which a

167

country is divided into large constituencies each returning several Members. Those candidates are elected who obtain more than a certain fraction of the vote, and their surplus votes over that fraction are distributed among the other candidates according to the second and later choices indicated on the ballot papers. As a result of this other candidates, whose votes then reach the required quota, are also elected. This is the method of the transferable vote.

Another method is that the votes given to a party in any constituency which are not sufficient for the election of a candidate are reserved, and these remainder votes from various constituencies are added up. If the total is sufficient for the election of one or more candidates, these are taken from a national list of the party, and the candidates become Members of Parliament without a constituency.

Ratification The action, by a state, of officially confirming a treaty signed by its representatives. It is effected by an exchange of documents, embodying their formal adoption of the treaty, between the states concerned. In the USA the power of ratification is vested in the President, subject to the advice and consent of the Senate. In the UK treaties are ratified by the Sovereign.

Referendum A reference of a particular political question to the electorate for a direct decision by direct popular vote. In many countries changes in the Constitution can only be made with the consent of the electorate obtained by this method.

Senate The Upper House of a bicameral legislature.

Separation of Powers The powers of government are threefold: legislative, executive, and judicial. Separation of powers implies that none of these is able to control or interfere with the others or that the same individuals

should not hold posts in more than one of the three branches, or that one branch of government should not exercise the functions of another.

Supreme Soviet The legislature of the USSR, comprising the Soviet of the Union and the Soviet of Nationalities.

168

Unicameral   Having or consisting of a single legislative Chamber.

Veto   The right to reject. The vested power or constitutional right of one branch or department of government, especially the chief executive, to reject a bill passed by a legislative body and thus prevent or delay its enactment into law.

Westminster, Statute of   An Act of Parliament of the UK, passed in 1931, defining the legislative powers of the Dominions of the former British Commonwealth, and giving statutory effect to resolutions passed by the Imperial Conferences held in 1926 and 1930. The Act abolished the remnants of Imperial legislative power but retained the Sovereign as the constitutional centre of the Commonwealth.